Smoking
THE ARTIFICIAL PASSION

Smoking

THE ARTIFICIAL PASSION

David Krogh

W. H. Freeman and Company

The excerpt on pages 1 and 2, "Introducing Tobacco to Civilization," from *The Button-Down Mind on TV* (Warner Brothers Records, 1962), is used by kind permission of Bob Newhart.

MELVYL is a registered trademark of the Regents of the University of California. MEDLINE is a registered trademark of the National Library of Medicine.

Library of Congress Cataloging-in-Publication Data

Krogh, David
   Smoking : the artificial passion / by David Krogh.
      p.   cm.
   Includes bibliographical references and index.
   ISBN 0-7167-2246-1
   1. Smoking. 2. Smoking—United States. I. Title.
   HV5733.K86   1991
   362.29'6—dc20   91-9789
                                                        CIP

Printed in the United States of America

1 2 3 4 5 6 7 8 9 0   VB   9 9 8 7 6 5 4 3 2 1

For my mother
and for the memory of my father

Contents

Foreword

Nicotine addiction, the world's number one public health enemy, causes two million preventable deaths each year. Smoking, the delivery system for nicotine, usually takes possession of its victims in their early teens and rapidly becomes an integral part of their styles of life. The popularity of smoking is understandable. Like no other mood-elevating drug, nicotine comes in a neat, readily accessible, inexpensive, legal vehicle—the cigarette. The very ritual of lighting up and smoking confers a sense of poise and security, and each cigarette reinforces the addiction by instant satisfaction of the smoker's craving. Unfortunately, while indulging in these pleasurable activities, the smoker is at the same time inhaling the carcinogens and other poisons that are the products of tobacco combustion.

As a surgeon in a large cancer hospital, where 30 percent of the adult patients are there because they smoked, I see the grim results of nicotine addiction in persons with cancers not only of the lung but of the mouth, larynx, esophagus, bladder, cervix, and kidney as well. Cancer specialists in general find that nine out of ten patients will stop smoking immediately upon hearing that they have a cancer caused by smoking. They will also confess that if, two weeks before the diagnosis, someone had told them they should stop, they would have found it impossible to do so. The remaining 10 percent are so shackled by nicotine that they will continue to smoke, even after surgery to remove, for instance, a cancerous lung or larynx. No more shocking example of the power of nicotine addiction exists than a patient who, with a permanent opening in his neck after removal of his larynx, devises a gadget that fits the opening and holds a cigarette.

Malignant disease is, of course, only one of the unhappy outcomes of smoking. Some victims of heart attacks, vascular disease, and emphysema, often the secondary results of smoking, cannot free themselves from the addiction either and continue smoking while a tube delivers oxygen to their failing lungs and hearts.

As a result of the widespread public education effort conducted in recent years, it is now generally known how hazardous smoking can be. Twenty million Americans have taken the hazards seriously enough to quit. However, some 50 million others continue to smoke. Three out of four smokers want to quit but find they cannot. What is the power of smoking that—despite information in the media, warnings on labels, advice of physicians and health workers, and pleas from friends and relatives—makes it seemingly impossible for smokers to give up their addiction?

In this book, David Krogh has distilled much of the vast amount of research that has been done on this drug that has such a widespread and devastating impact. He lucidly recounts the complex physiological and psychological elements of addiction. He deals with questions of whether "nicomaniacs" are genetically predisposed to their addiction, of whether extroverts or introverts are more likely to become smokers and less likely to be able to quit, and about the role of social mores in perpetuating tobacco addiction. He discusses what some researchers believe are centers in the brain for the impulsive or compulsive behavior of addiction, not just to nicotine but to other drugs as well. (What immediately suggests itself is that a drug or other device that would act on these centers so as to control the "artificial passion" would be one of the truly great contributions to human health and longevity.)

Krogh does not go through a laundry list of the methods that smokers have used to quit, some successful, some not. Instead, he skillfully uses the current knowledge about nicotine's effects to account for the difficulties smokers have in quitting. He makes the important point that those who try to quit and relapse should not be discouraged or feel guilty, because learning to quit, like other sorts of learning, often benefits from repetition, and experience teaches the ways to avoid the traps that cause relapses.

Krogh suggests that nicotine chewing gum might succeed where other methods do not. A chiclet in place of a cigarette can provide the small doses of nicotine that the smoker's body craves, thereby reducing the acute, often unrelenting symptoms brought on by abrupt withdrawal. (Those symptoms, incidentally, distinguish an addiction from a habit.) The gum also breaks the ritual of selecting a cigarette from the package, tapping it once or twice, inserting it in the mouth, reaching for a match, and lighting up. Having avoided the carcinogens, smokers will often become dependent upon the fix they obtain from the gum and will remain attached to it for many months. Still, if it breaks the ritual of smoking, it is worth the dependency.

Krogh presents his scholarly analysis of the complex mechanism of nicotine addiction in a highly readable, often witty style. Like Lewis Thomas, he both delights and educates. Ex-smokers will be fascinated by the insights into what motivated them to start smoking and what made it so difficult to stop. Smokers who are eager to quit will be enlightened about the processes responsible for the relentless force that goads them on. By no means the least of the book's virtues will be its service as a valuable reference for health educators and anti-tobacco activists. And, of course, the book will appeal to cancer experts, cardiologists, obstetricians, pediatricians, and lung specialists who are constantly confronted with the end results of the artificial passion. I am certain that, like me, these physicians will be grateful to David Krogh for helping them understand the many elements responsible for what Charles Lemaistre, past president of the American Cancer Society, has called "one of the most grievous examples of destructive behavior in the history of mankind."

William G. Cahan, M.D.

Preface

The question of why people smoke interested me initially because of the paradox it set before me. To my way of thinking, smoking and its motivations seemed rather like a large blue elephant in the middle of the living room that was being ignored, oddly enough, by everyone present.

At that time—now several years ago—I thought: Here is this practice that is expensive and dirty *and deadly,* and that stretches to every corner of the earth and further back in time than some religions, but it's not clear why anybody does it. Furthermore, nobody seems mystified by this lack of understanding. If millions of Americans suddenly began standing around exhaust pipes regularly to get a lung full of bad air, there would be widespread interest in the reasons for this behavior. But it seemed to me that smoking—no less irrational on the face of it—did not inspire much curiosity simply because it's been around so long and in so many places.

Smokers I talked to certainly didn't have a handle on their habit; it was a mystery to them how they could be pulled into place at predictable intervals so that the ritual of tobacco inhalation and exhalation could proceed. Their inarticulateness extended even to the periods when they were most aware of smoking's proddings: when they were trying to quit. I'd see them a week or two weeks or a month after their effort had begun, by which time they'd be smoking again, and learn that they went back to it because . . . well, because there was something about it that they just *couldn't do without*.

If there had been nothing more to it than this, I probably would have just shrugged my shoulders and continued to wonder at the odd ways of human beings. But, of course, there's the matter of the *effects* of this strange practice, by which I mean the almost unbelievable carnage that stems from it. Of all the statistics that exist about smoking, here is one to keep: 1,000 Americans will die from it today. Smoking will kill more Americans this year (and next, and next) than AIDS, heroin, crack cocaine, alcohol, car accidents, fire, and murder combined, as a U.S. public health official observed recently. No other act in the everyday behavior of Americans can touch it as a grim reaper.

Against this, we can celebrate a remarkable change that has come about recently in the smoking habits of middle-class Americans: smoking is disappearing from their offices, their trains, their restaurants, their friends' homes—in short, from their lives entirely. This change can truly be described as revolutionary since, to my knowledge, it has no precedent in history anywhere on earth.

A shift of this magnitude may breed a false sense, however, that smoking is about to disappear altogether—from America if not from the world. What is actually happening is that smoking is disappearing from one group in one country. Even in the United States, our best estimates are that by the year 2000, about 22 percent of all adult Americans will be smoking (down from about 27 percent today). And in most of the rest of the world, smoking rates are going up, not down. Given this, smoking's huge toll will continue well into the 21st century.

These figures, and the mystery I've described, combined several years ago to make me begin poring over the mountain of scientific literature that exists on the reasons for smoking. What I hope I've retrieved from this tonnage is a narrative that helps explain to the average person why people use tobacco. Providing this kind of explanation is at least the nominal goal of this book, but, as will become apparent, this is very much a book about drug use in general. Imbedded in my coverage of *this* as a subject are primers on such topics as the human nervous system, personality, and genetics, which I think will make the trip through these pages more rewarding.

Beyond these things, there is a higher level lesson to be had here, I believe, about the kinds of physical and psychological states that human beings find attractive. I think that we are, at root, less interested in the exotic than in the normal. Our chief concern is not with how we can *transform* ourselves for discrete periods of time, but rather with how we can remain the same. What is remarkable is the peril we are willing to take on in order to do this.

I have cleaved to the scientific paradigm in these pages as if no other explanatory system existed. There are undoubtedly mythological, folk, and literary accounts of the motivations behind smoking, but the reader won't find them here. I've assumed that anything we can really *know* about a subject like smoking can come only by running it through the wringer of science. I have not hesitated to speculate on many things in connection with smoking, but I have tried to label my guesswork as just that.

Some of the book's material—where a scientist found this, when he did that—may be a little thick, but my advice is: stay with it; perseverance will pay off. When I say in the text that somebody discovered something in a particular year, that should be understood to mean that a scientific paper on that topic was published in that year. Where scientific evidence competes, I have often jettisoned the back-and-forth of dispute in favor of presenting an account of the side that I believe has won, at least for the time being.

The title of this book comes from John Quincy Adams who, in 1845, wrote a letter to a Rev. Samuel H. Cox in Brooklyn, who was then preparing an introduction to a book on "Tobacco and its mysteries." Adams related how, as a young man, he had been addicted to smoking and chewing but resolved to quit, and after a difficult struggle of about three months, he felt himself free of tobacco's grip.

"I have often wished," he said, "that every individual . . . afflicted with this artificial passion could force it upon himself to try but for three months the experiment which I made, sure that it would turn every acre of tobacco land into a wheat field, and add five years to the average of human life." Noble sentiments, then and now.

• • •

This book was produced the old-fashioned way: without benefit of grants, sabbaticals, or leaves of absence. There are, however, some *individuals* who have been helpful in this project, and I would like to thank them here. The first of them are MELVYL and MEDLINE— brothers, in the sense that they are two computer databases at the University of California libraries. Though somewhat aloof in their manner, they were tireless in their assistance and indispensable to this work. Corless Smith, Neil Smelser, Jerry Keleher, and Jed Rose provided detailed constructive criticism and encouragement, which I very much appreciated. Many thanks to Diana Siemens for her sensitive editing of the manuscript. Reference Librarian Barbara Glendenning was extremely helpful with research techniques. The federal Office on Smoking and Health provided a wealth of bibliographic information. A number of scientists working in the field made themselves available for long conversations about drug research; I would particularly like to single out Jack Henningfield and Roy Wise in this regard. Tom Wangerin's counsel was invaluable. Finally, thanks to Joseph Ewing at W. H. Freeman and Company, who believed in this book, and to Anne Marshall, who believed in my ability to produce it.

David Krogh
Kensington, California
May 1991

Smoking
THE ARTIFICIAL PASSION

One may say that true life begins where the tiny bit begins—where what seem to us minute and infinitely small alterations take place. True life is not lived where great external changes take place—where people move about, clash, fight, and slay one another—it is lived only where these tiny, tiny, infinitesimally small changes occur.

—TOLSTOY

CHAPTER 1

Why Do People Do That?

I have known Spaniards, on the island of Hispaniola, who were accustomed to taking [cigars] and who, being reproved and told that this was a vice, replied that they were not able to stop. . . . I do not know what pleasure or advantage they find in them.
—BARTOLOME DE LAS CASAS, 1527[1]

ONE OF WESTERN culture's longest running bewilderments may have been stated first by De Las Casas, the great humanitarian of the period when the Old World was conquering the New. What, he wondered, is the attraction of these *smouldering weeds,* that people should covet their smoke as if it were the breath of life itself?

Five hundred years after the tobacco genie was let out of the bottle and into Western life, there still is a bafflement about smoking, one that spills over occasionally into derision or even anger. (The 19th-century American Horace Greeley once defined a cigar as "a fire at one end and a fool at the other.")[2]

When he was first doing stand-up comedy, Bob Newhart would begin one of his best bits by noting that "It seems to me that the uses of tobacco aren't obvious right off the bat." He then imagined a 17th-century phone call between Sir Walter Raleigh and the head of the "West

Indies Company" in London, with Raleigh explaining this newfound substance to his boss. You could take this tobacco, the boss was told, shred it up, put it on a piece of paper, and:

> Then what do you do to it, Walt? (Laughs) You set fire to it, Walt? (Laughs) Then what do you do, Walt? You *inhale the smoke.* You know, Walt, it seems, off-hand, like you could stand in front of your fireplace and have the same thing going for you. . . . I think you're going to have a tough time, ahh, selling people on sticking burning leaves in their mouths.[3]

Not so tough a time at all, as it turns out. Even today, however, with centuries of cultural tradition behind it, tobacco still puzzles. The vast majority of nonsmokers think that smoking has the dubious distinction of not providing much pleasure but being addictive all the same.[4]

Smokers themselves, understandably, tend to see the habit in less negative terms. Only about half of them regard themselves as addicted, and they're apt to describe smoking in terms of pleasure[5]—usually as a matter of smoking "calming" them. Yet even smokers seem to have fairly hazy notions of what benefits smoking provides. Britain's M. A. H. Russell, who has spent a good part of his working life trying to understand the smoking habit, puts it this way:

> To seek the solution to the question, why do people smoke?, the obvious way to begin would seem to be simply to ask; but if we do this we soon discover that many smokers are at a loss for a satisfactory answer. . . . When confronted with this question they hesitate, smile foolishly, shrug their shoulders and say something like, "Habit I suppose," or "I don't know." . . . The simple answer is that they enjoy it, but the simple pleasure principle does not always operate with smoking. There are few who positively enjoy every cigarette and some smokers experience no positive pleasure at all.[6]

So what *does* tobacco do? With its use, there's none of heroin's ecstasy, alcohol's sudden brightening of personality, marijuana's giddiness, LSD's visions. The urge to get high is understandable, even to those who disdain it. But what's to be made of tobacco smoking? To the casual, nonsmoking observer, it's as if smokers have gotten the worst of both worlds: drug addiction without drug euphoria.

Yet smoking's nebulous benefits come attached to a habit of amazing power. Ninety percent of all drinkers drink alcohol when they feel like it but leave it alone when they don't, which leaves about 10 percent drinking out of compulsion. These percentages are almost exactly reversed with smoking: only about 10 percent of the smoking population are thought to be "chippers," who can take smoking or leave it as they please. The Smoking Nag must be served at regular intervals for 90 percent of the smoking population, and this population amounts to better than one in four adult Americans. Since smokers take about 10 drags per cigarette, a pack-a-day habit, which is about the average, adds up to 200 "hits" of tobacco per day—or about 70,000 hits annually. The number is easy to calculate because there are no vacations from the practice.

Who can comprehend the effect of a habit this constant? Smoking is the familiar tug on the sleeve: at the office, at the dinner table, in the car, in front of the television. Observe smokers at the intermission of a play, rushing to light up as the crowd files out or hungrily taking a last drag before Act II begins. Kept from their normal smoking cycle—about one cigarette every 40 minutes—they need a quick infusion of smoke to keep the Nag at bay. This goes on in less noticeable form all day, every day, for the vast majority of smokers. Smoking may be pleasurable in some instances, but certainly is a necessity in others. In these latter cases, smoking has first call on the smoker's activities. Neither work nor play can go forward unhindered until the Nag is served. So deeply does smoking work itself into the warp and weft of human behavior that one can seriously begin to ask to what degree lifestyle creates occasions for smoking or smoking creates lifestyle.

How amazing, then, that smokers have so little idea of why they do it. Smoking seems to sit, fat and laughing, on one of our cherished assumptions: that we have *reasons* for doing what we do; that we are purposeful even in our indulgences. People often do things they don't understand, but what comes close to smoking in terms of an ongoing act that is motivated by forces that are within us, and yet unknown to us? At the conference table of the self, smoking speaks another language; it takes up our time and energy, but is unable to tell us why. If smoking's consequences were benign, its constancy—hour after hour, day after day—would be noteworthy enough. That its consequences are deadly, but its purpose unknown, should make us make us very curious about what is at work here.

The landmark Surgeon General's report of 1964—the first one on tobacco—said that smoking was "habituating" but not "addicting." Tobacco's use, the report said, was related primarily to "psychological and social drives" that were reinforced by the effects of nicotine. In retrospect, we can see that the 1964 report lies near the beginning of modern scientific research into why people smoke. (This is natural enough, since the report itself brought urgency to the issue.) Since that time, there have been thousands of scientific investigations into the subject, with research going, in a general way, from a "softer," psychological approach to a "harder" approach that places more emphasis on biological processes and pharmacology. This work has borne considerable fruit, particularly in the 1980s, and not just on theoretical issues. In the words of Jerome Jaffe of the National Institute on Drug Abuse, smoking research has "shipped."[7] It has delivered a product— nicotine gum—that seems to be of real value, at least in helping people get over early withdrawal symptoms when they quit smoking.

The gum could stand, however, both as a symbol of how far smoking research has come and how far it has to go. Despite its value, nicotine gum is not the magic bullet against smoking that we all might hope for: the substance that, once ingested, would allow anyone to quit smoking quickly and painlessly. Even with it, quitting frequently is so difficult that it makes smokers ask the question of the infirm: How long must I feel this bad?

Smoking research is definitely work in progress. There are a multitude of unanswered questions in the field, and the research results that are obtained often are maddeningly contradictory. Nevertheless, a clearer picture of why people smoke has emerged in recent years, and this work, as we will see, provides some insight into the question of drug use in general.

The central finding of contemporary scientific research on smoking is straightforward, stands in contradiction to the 1964 Surgeon General's report, and pretty much confirms what generations of preachers and grandmothers have suspected: people smoke primarily to get nicotine into their bodies. There are other reasons for smoking, as we'll see, but alone or together it's unlikely that they could motivate millions of people to regularly draw a somewhat bitter pollutant into their lungs. M. A. H. Russell puts it this way:

> There is little doubt that if it were not for the nicotine in tobacco smoke, people would be little more inclined to smoke than they are to blow bubbles or to light sparklers.[8]

Readers may be inclined at this point to say that they knew this all along and to ask why the government has spent so much of their money trying to confirm it. Let me quickly point out, then, that there is a universe of meaning in the phrase "primarily to get nicotine into their bodies," and that, therefore, some serious misunderstanding may result.

The likely confusion is that people are apt to think that this explanation of smoking means nothing more than that people are addicted to nicotine. To further compound the trouble, the average person is likely to have a misguided notion of what "addiction" means.

The common understanding of addiction is of a one-dimensional craving for a drug: a mental and physical discomfort—perhaps even anguish—that must be endured until more of the drug is taken or the addiction is shaken off. We might call this a "monkey addiction," since it could just as well be monkeys we're talking about, there being no *human* quality to the act under this view. Give drug X to an organism for long enough and the organism will become addicted to it, after which it will have to have a certain amount of the drug running around in its system or suffer the consequences.

Note that what's implied here is a kind of thermostat for an addictive drug: for smokers a nic-o-stat, regulating nicotine; for, say, heroin users a morphine-o-stat. When the amount of the drug in the system gets low, the stat kicks in, distress follows, and more of the drug must be taken.

Now, monkey addiction requires only that the nicotine tank be kept full to a certain level. Smokers trying to quit will soon go below this level. (They will reach the "dose-needed" stage.) Thereafter, their need should be a simple function of "drug-supplied or drug-denied." Given this, their propensity to relapse shouldn't change depending on the circumstances they find themselves in. But this is precisely what we do *not* find with cigarettes. We have no reason to believe that smokers relapse in accordance with some chemical clock. They relapse when they get bad news, when they're stressed, or when they're at a party. They relapse after they've had a good dinner.[9]

If a monkey addiction theory is true, why should a smoker's internal state or external surroundings prompt relapse? If we stretch the theory, we might be able to accommodate depressive states. ("The need was constant, but I only gave into it when work got me down.") But what about relaxing or exuberant states, which also are a minefield for people trying to quit? Moreover, with monkey addiction, we would presume that withdrawal symptoms—irritability, confusion, and so forth—would be the thing that would prompt an ex-smoker to light up again. But Saul Shiffman, who is one of the nation's leading experts in this area, has studied a large number of relapse crises in ex-smokers and reported that a majority of these episodes occur in the absence of withdrawal symptoms.[10]

Finally, consider the role of nicotine gum. Presumably, it should take care of the nic-o-stat. If monkey addiction were a correct model, we would expect this oral replenishment of the drug to eliminate cigarette withdrawal symptoms. In high enough doses, the gum does this to a large extent—irritability, anxiety, and difficulty in concentrating, for example, all are lessened with it. But one symptom remains that is so overriding, it seems to make a mockery of the gum's good effects. What the gum doesn't wipe out is the urge to smoke. If monkey addiction were true, shouldn't this urge simply be the sum total of all the other withdrawal symptoms? If we take care of them with the gum, what is this thing that remains?

The problem with the common understanding of cigarette addiction is that it doesn't begin to tell us *enough* about why people engage in a behavior that they know stands a good chance of sending them to an early grave. Cigarette smoking does have an element of monkey addiction in it—something that we might do better to call "physical dependence," as scientists do. But that's not all there is to it. In the broadest of terms, what's wrong with this view of smoking is that it sees the cigarette habit as a purely pharmacological process. That in itself is off the mark, but there's a compound error in monkey addiction: it posits a chemical habit that is all stick and no carrot; it says that smokers who try to quit are physically punished—and that's why they keep smoking.

As we will see, however, there are abundant reasons to believe that cigarettes do things *for* smokers as well as *to* them. This duality exists with all addictive drugs, but may be somewhat harder to see with cigarettes. With, say, cocaine or alcohol, we have no problem perceiving their apparent reward: users get high from them. What about smoking? The problem in seeing the commonality between cigarettes and other drugs comes because of our preconceived notions of what addictive drugs do.

We need to grasp the fact that a drug can be desirable to people without making them euphoric. It can be rewarding without getting us "high" as that term is commonly understood. Most of the addictive drugs we know about *other* than cigarettes have an apparent element of euphoria to their use. What's important to recognize, however, is that being blissed-out is only one of many ways in which drugs can be rewarding. Being mildly stimulated or tranquilized is another. Nicotine seems to be able to do both things, and these are a couple of the reasons it's attractive.

Indeed, subtle effects of this sort may be very great attractions. We recognize this with alcohol: it's the soothing reward of having just one drink. Might not there be the same, or even greater, value in a drug that is taken *strictly* for subtle effects? If we think about it for a second, why should we assume that being *dramatically* altered by a drug would be more attractive to the average person than being *slightly* altered? Most people assume, I think, that the more dramatic a drug's effect, the more attractive it would be to anyone; that if any of us encountered heroin, for example, we would find it so overwhelmingly attractive we would want to continue with it forever.

But we have good reason to believe that this is not the case at all. As Jack Henningfield of the National Institute on Drug Abuse says: "If we tested heroin and we just picked 50 people up off the street, and gave them doses of heroin, most of them would get sick and they wouldn't like it."[11] What matters is not so much whether people get *smashed* on a drug; what matters is whether they find the drug *useful:* for relaxing, for remaining alert, for working, for imagining—or for getting blissed-out.

Now if people find a mildly tranquilizing drug useful and take it for long enough, and then that drug isn't available to them anymore, there's a possibility that in their "withdrawal" from the drug there will be an element of physical dependence—manifested as an unpleasant physical state.

But isn't there likely to be something else, too, something a little less exotic, but perhaps important in its own way? Won't they simply *miss* not having that mild tranquilizer around whenever they want it? This is not something we can measure in terms of heart beats per minute or brain-wave states. But isn't it likely to affect our behavior?

A person raised in coastal Maine but now living in Kansas may miss the ocean—may miss it to the point of returning to Maine even though he or she has a better job in Kansas. We can't describe that person as being "addicted" to the ocean, unless the term is to lose all its meaning. Yet this person's attachment to the sea has caused him to act, in one sense, against his own best interests. There is surely some of this with cigarettes, or for that matter with any addictive drug we know about. We are attached to their effects as well as addicted to them; we feel an absence when these effects are no longer at our disposal. In this sense, drug use—commonly cordoned off in our minds to a separate, dark underworld—is not so much different from any number of other things in our lives.

If it's possible to miss having a mild tranquilizer, is it not possible to miss something simply *connected* to having it—say, holding a cigarette? Pack-a-day smokers hold them 140 times a week. And they hold them on many of these occasions at very specified times—after a meal, while filling out reports at work, while doing the crossword puzzle. After a time, wouldn't manipulating the cigarette while doing the crossword become nearly as reflexive as shifting in the chair while working on it?

Readers may be able to see where I'm going with all this. We have seen the reasons for smoking start with physical punishment for *not* smoking; then we added pharmacological rewards *for* smoking; then we speculated on the personal, almost emotional, nature of *missing* a pharmacological effect; then we talked about missing a smoking-related behavior that has nothing directly to do with pharmacology at all.

If all these things are motivations for smoking, then the seemingly simple act of drawing tobacco smoke into the lungs—this *nothing* activity, so slight it's hardly there—begins to be seen for what it is: a habit of deep roots and great complexity. As we will see, addiction and attachment; pharmacology and behavior; personality, culture, and genetics all chase each other around like a cat after its own tail when we start to consider the issue of why people smoke.

That said, we should remember how this discussion started: with the assertion that the main reason people smoke is to get nicotine into their bodies. This is true not only because of the direct effects nicotine has, but because of its indirect effects. Think of the four reasons I set forth for smoking. The first two—being physically rewarded for smoking or physically punished for not smoking—clearly are pharmacological effects. But what about the other two reasons? (Chosen almost at random, by the way; many others could have been selected.) Well, *missing* having a mild tranquilizer around is not a matter of physical dependence, but it is *based* on the pharmacological effects of nicotine. The fourth reason follows this pattern as well. The reason people get used to holding cigarettes is not that this act is pleasurable in itself. We have no instances of people taking up tobacco *holding*. They take up tobacco smoking (and only later, when they're trying to quit, do we find them regularly holding unlit cigarettes). It is the pairing of nicotine's effects with holding that gives the latter act its power.

The point here is that nicotine is like a stone dropped in a pond: it has direct effects and indirect effects. A water strider might be sunk by such a stone or buffeted by the ripples that its splash creates. But ultimately, there is one cause for all the effects.

This analogy is not exact. There are reasons for smoking that lie completely outside the effects of nicotine. Some of these may be strong motivating forces. But science increasingly points to nicotine as the strongest force of all in motivating smoking. Before turning to its role in the smoking habit, however, we might benefit from taking a look at some motivations for smoking that are related only weakly, if at all, to this subtle yet powerful drug in tobacco.

CHAPTER 2

Outside the Chemical Realm

THERE MAY BE a few Americans—but only a few—who have a childhood distant enough that they can recall a time when the spittoon and the cigar were as common a sight as the cigarette. Because cigarettes claim 95 percent of the tobacco market in the United States today, it's easy to assume that they have always accounted for the lion's share of sales, but that's not the case. The cigarette's ascendence didn't begin until the late 19th century, and its triumph in America wasn't complete until the 1920s. Pipes, cigars, snuff, and chewing tobacco have all competed for center stage at different times or places in the world.* (See footnote on next page.)

One of the notable shifts in forms of tobacco use came in England in the 18th century when snuff replaced the pipe, at least among the upper classes. This led the literary figure Samuel Johnson to complain to his biographer Boswell in 1773 that

> Smoaking has gone out. To be sure, it is a shocking thing, blowing smoak out of our mouths into other peoples mouths, eyes, and noses, and having the same thing done to us. Yet I cannot account why a thing which requires so little exertion, and yet preserves the mind from total vacuity, should have gone out.[1]

I think Johnson was on to something there. To put his statement about exertion and vacuity another way, we might say that in the right circumstances, smoking is about as close as a person can come to doing nothing while still doing something. Though we may not like to admit it, this kind of minimalism can be very attractive. It is one of the attractions of television. Human beings may be incapable of doing absolutely nothing, but they don't mind coming close, and smoking can fit into this narrow space quite well. The lighting and stubbing of the cigarette; the slight manipulation of it; the languorous exhalation of smoke toward the ceiling—these are the relaxing, almost comforting, acts that smoking can provide. They're often accompanied by the visual entertainment of clouds of smoke, and an energy surge in this state can lead to smoking's superb artistic creation, the smoke ring.

The something side of smoking can be helpful when nothing is what's called for in a given situation. William Hunt and Joseph Matarazzo point out that smoking a cigarette while, for example, waiting for a friend,

> not only permits activity, but also seems a more logical, purposeful, and dignified activity than pacing back and forth or standing in one place tapping one's foot or twirling one's hat.[2]

This points us in the direction of a more general use of smoking: it can be a valuable communication tool. Those who wish to project an

---

*Note that these four forms present three different means of getting tobacco into the system. Over the centuries, people have managed to use nearly every conceivable human orifice as a tobacco portal, if not for pleasure, then in medicinal applications. This fact prompted one Hans Jakob von Grimmelshausen to harrumph in 1667, near the dawn of German tobacco use, that some people "drink their tobacco, some eat it, others sniff it up through the nostrils—indeed, I am surprised that I have not yet found anyone plugging his ears with it."[3]

image or signal something about themselves to the outside world have a great communication device in the cigarette. This is most obvious in societal caricatures: Marlene Dietrich exhaling sensually; Edward Murrow looking thoughtful. (Note that these examples must be drawn from the past; who among today's public figures wears smoking emblematically, as these people did? Famous people still smoke, but now they hide the fact.)

There also are more subtle forms of communication with smoking, however. There is, for example, what we might call dismissive exhalation: the brief spout of smoke sent quickly skyward with head upturned before talking is resumed, the whole act bespeaking a busy, tightly controlled self. Propriety can be signaled too. When I was in college, sorority girls at dining tables smoked in a precisely defined way. They always *held* the cigarette in hand while lighting it and in between puffs cocked the left wrist outward, extended the fingers slightly, and pointed the cigarette to 10 o'clock. Their act, then as now slightly suspect, was balanced with a body language that exuded rectitude. They even sat up straight.

It is the other side of this coin, however, that smoking is better known for. Smoking is not often a sexually alluring act; indeed, it is so infrequently this that I've sometimes suspected that actors may be the only people capable of making it one. But when it is sexually charged, it can be very effective—the best example I know being the young Lauren Bacall dangling a fat cigarette from her lips while talking to Bogart.

When we ask why smoking is capable of exciting us sexually, the obvious answer is that it looks like fellatio. This is true enough and it's the reason, I would imagine, that smoking's sexual aura burns more intensely around women than men. (And comes solely in connection with cigarettes, the only thing women smoke en masse. Cigars obviously are a much more suitable phallic substitute, but the sex meter stays near zero when men smoke them; pipes are less than zero on the scale.)

There are other reasons for associating smoking with sexuality, however. One of these is that, more than any other act, perhaps, smoking draws our attention to that seat of sensuousness, the lips. Programmed as we are to follow any visual stimulus, we track the smoker's ostentatious act to its stopping point and find ourselves looking, however briefly, at a mouth in action.

Beyond this, sex is, of course, intimately entwined with our notions of need and the desire for a forbidden object. Smoking is, and has been for centuries, an *advertisement* of need. Its object—drug-induced contentment—is as indecent as sex. Smokers and lovers alike are perceived as people driven by illicit urges beyond their control. They are people who, in consuming their exotic, dangerous objects, are themselves consumed. The intertwining of sex and smoking in this way has its perfect expression in Lawrence Kasdan's movie *Body Heat,* where William Hurt and Kathleen Turner smoke and copulate as if both acts were driven by some single, underlying need that only grows greater by being served. We will see later that the kinds of people who smoke give us an additional reason for linking sex and cigarettes. It seems to me, however, that image alone is enough to bond the two together.

Image expression is based, of course, on self-image, in which cigarettes seem to play a part. In 1971, Bernard Mausner and Ellen Platt found that a majority of the adult smokers they surveyed in an experiment agreed that a picture of themselves with a cigarette showed "the real me," whereas a picture without a cigarette did not.[4]

It should not surprise us that smokers may be seeking to alter "the real me" along some predictable lines. In 1967 John Weir photographed four adolescent male models posed with cigarettes and then made retouched photographs that kept the models but did away with all signs of them smoking. He then provided a group of several hundred teenage boys with different versions of the pictures and a list of 80 adjectives that could be used to describe the models. The with-cigarette pictures prompted the boys to describe the models more often as "adventurous," "daring," and "masculine" and less often as "timid."[5]

What's apparent, of course, is that the adventurous adjectives evoked by the picture of the smoking models are precisely the adjectives that Marlboro, for example, would like to evoke in readers when it shows them pictures of the Marlboro Cowboy looking pensively at Montana. A chicken-and-egg question arises as to whether advertising has *created* the association between adventurousness, etc., and smoking or whether advertising is responding to an already existing association between the two.

Each element has undoubtedly reinforced the other, but we have reason to believe that advertising is responding more than creating.

Smoking has always been somewhat daring and has become much more so since the 1960s. And, as we will see later, a particular sort of daring and individualistic person is inordinately attracted to smoking; cigarette companies know this and cigarette advertising images are the result. With these ads pasted on billboards all over town, millions of youngsters have a ready-made avenue for their rebellious urges. There's a commercially approved way of being daring and it's called smoking cigarettes.

It's a common observation that smokers are heavily represented in certain desk-bound professions, such as journalism or accounting. Since smoking currently is getting booted out of the white-collar world altogether, this phenomenon is waning, but it's still worth asking if there are any reasons—apart from the effects of nicotine—for the connection between smoking and this kind of work. I believe so, in that carrying out tasks in these kinds of jobs demands the suppression of what Isidor Chein has called "divergent activities."

A writer in an office who begins a paragraph must filter out internal or external diversions in order to complete it. There's talk, noise, machine clatter. In addition, the difficulty of writing often propels the writer in the direction of other activities—of leaning back, of opening the window, of reviewing what he's already written. (It's as if writers have to make several assaults on the expression of complex thoughts; they're likely to be thrown into window-staring on the first try or two as if they had bounced off a sumo wrestler.) As Chein points out, smoking is able to harness this kind of divergent energy. Smoking is such a routinized activity that smokers don't have to think about doing it. Because it allows for movement without the expenditure of psychological energy, it provides, as Chein says, "an innocuous channel for wandering attention."[6]

If the average person has an opinion as to the reasons people smoke *aside* from nicotine addiction, he or she is likely to say that people want something to do with their hands. This could be looked at simply as one kind of divergent activity in the family Chein is talking about.

If conventional Freudian wisdom has filtered down to our person on the street, he or she might add that smokers want something to do with their mouths as well, smokers perhaps being "orally fixated." This latter view has had its highbrow advocates. W. H. Auden's place among the century's great poets may not yet be settled, but he certainly ranks as one of the century's great smokers. ("Everything he touches turns to cigarettes," complained his friend Louis MacNeice.)[7] Auden in his younger days said that his burdensome habit resulted from "insufficient weaning. I must have something to suck."[8]

This sounds like something Freud himself would have come up with, but as it turns out, Freud puts a slightly different spin on things. For him, the sucking of the *thumb* as a baby is a sexual act that some children are destined to get more out of than others (as their lips and mouths serve as more intense "erotogenic" zones). If these children persist with this kind of intensified oral gratification, as adults they "will become epicures in kissing, will be inclined to perverse kissing, or, if males, will have a powerful motive for drinking and smoking," he says.[9] As is so often the case with Freud, we're expected to take his word for all this, as he offers no evidence in support of it.

The zoologist Desmond Morris has pointed out, somewhat more sensibly, that "having something between the lips is a comforting experience for the human animal," as evidenced by the fact, he says, that studies of infant pacifiers show that they dramatically reduce crying and general agitation in babies.[10] As for the child, so for the man or woman, Morris says. Culture, alas, will not permit adults to go around with pacifiers in their mouths. The cigarette is an understandable substitute but it has the unfortunate side effect of killing people.

Morris makes the argument that an "oral" motivation for smoking should be nearly universal in human beings. If this is true, we might guess that those people who actually become smokers would differ in "orality" in some ways from nonsmokers. When we turn to actual experiments on the subject, we find a mixed bag that offers some support for a slightly different version of this proposition.

In 1958, Charles McArthur and his colleagues at Harvard found that, among a group of 252 Harvard men they followed for about 15 years, the ability of smokers to *stop* smoking was directly related to how long they had been—brace yourself for this—breast-fed as babies. The longer their time on the teat, the more likely it was that they would be able to quit. For example, light smokers who could stop were weaned at an average of 8 months; heavy smokers who could stop were weaned at 6.8 months; and other smokers (mostly heavy) who tried to stop but couldn't were weaned at 4.7 months.[11] Interestingly, McArthur found no clear-cut difference between smokers and lifelong nonsmokers as to how long they had been breast-fed.

Michael Howe and Angela Summerfield did some similar work in 1979 with a study that looked at such "orality differences" as nail-biting and thumb- or candy-sucking. Again, they found no differences between smokers and nonsmokers: members of both groups, for example, bit their nails with the same frequency and had enjoyed licorice sticks as children in about the same proportion. The researchers did, however, find differences among two groups of *smokers:* those who, in the past, had quit for at least a year and those who had never managed it for more than three months. The "continuous" smokers were more oral in general than the quitters. Likewise, those who smoked for reasons like "craving" or "habit" were more oral than those who reported smoking for social reasons.[12]

In between these two studies, there have been at least five other investigations of this general topic. Looked at in overview, this work provides some support for a connection between orality and smoking, but we need to read the fine print here. The link established that seems most secure is between orality and *heavy,* habit smoking, rather than between orality and the initiation of smoking.

Social critics are fond of saying that we live in an age in which image is paramount and style is more important than substance. If so, cigarette advertising could stand as a perfect symbol of its time in that it has everything to do with image and almost nothing to do with the substance of its product. What is promoted in cigarette ads are dreams: of cowboys or glamorous women or fun days with friends. These dreams are then linked to specific brands: Marlboros or Virginia Slims or Newports. American advertising in general is heavy on image, of course, but few products can run with cigarettes in this regard. (Soft-drink and liquor ads come to mind; perhaps it is that the more useless or dangerous the product, the more advertising for it will be based on pure image.)

When cigarette ads do deign to come down to the fuddy-duddy world of product *qualities,* only three things are of any importance: tar and nicotine ratings for "light" brands; price for "generic" brands; and taste for many different brands. It's the last of these that concerns us here. If there is any "sensible" reason that people can put forward for smoking, this is it. Nearly all the other reasons, if expressed, stand to expose some element of human frailty or incompleteness in the smoker. Everyone is incomplete and frail, of course, but the smoker goes *public* with this fact every time he lights up. This has always been true to some extent, but is especially so now. Addiction, compulsion, irrational action: these are the messages that waft up with the smoke.

The fact that taste stands nearly alone in being an unassailable motive for smoking is, I would guess, one of the reasons that cigarette companies make as much of it as they do in their advertising. It helps take them out of the world of drug-dealing by making them seem more like regular companies that cater to the public taste in the same way that, say, gum manufacturers do.

On the other hand, the tobacco firms' interest in taste clearly extends beyond image and public relations. Dozens of patents may be granted in a given year for tobacco "flavorants," which often have names like 2,6,6-trimethyl-1-(3-ethoxy-1-butenyl)-cyclohex-1-ene.[13] These chemicals are put into cigarettes alongside more familiar flavorings, such as sugar, licorice, and vanilla. Flavorings, in turn, are only one kind of additive in a product that's full of them.*

The mix of flavorings in any given brand of cigarettes is among the most tightly held secrets tobacco companies have, and trade journals tell us that flavorants have become more important in recent years because of the difficulty manufacturers have in making low-tar and nicotine cigarettes palatable.[14]

---

* The Food and Drug Administration normally must pass judgment on synthetic substances added to products that Americans put in their bodies, but this rule has been bypassed with tobacco. When the FDA was set up at the turn of the century, tobacco was ruled by Congress to be neither food nor drug, and this absurd premise has remained in place to this day, thanks to the political might of the tobacco lobby. Thus tobacco and all that goes in it is outside FDA jurisdiction.

With the passage of the Comprehensive Smoking Prevention Education Act of 1984, however, tobacco companies had to begin supplying to the federal Office on Smoking and Health (OSH) lists of all additives that go into cigarettes. The lists are turned over in such a way that neither cigarette brands nor companies can be identified with particular additives. (The "big six" cigarette manufacturers turn their lists over to a Washington law firm, Covington and Burling, which then supplies a unitary list to OSH.) The

All in all, then, one gets the sense that tobacco companies believe that flavor matters a good deal to their customers. Whatever else these companies are, they're not dumb, and we probably should accept their efforts at flavoring cigarettes as a sign that flavor does make a difference—at least as to what brand of cigarettes smokers choose. When we look at the research on this subject that's not locked in corporate vaults, however, we're left with the impression that there is a lot of play in smokers' judgments about tobacco taste.

One of the few experiments in tobacco research literature that deserves to be called venerable was done by psychologist Clark Hull at the University of Wisconsin in 1924. Hull blindfolded his subjects and provided them with a specially prepared pipe that delivered not tobacco smoke, but warm, moist air. Then, standing nearby and smoking a lit pipe of his own, he could fool these men into thinking they were smoking when in fact they were just puffing on heated air. One man, he reported, serenely went through the motions of blowing smoke rings in this condition.[15]

Through the early 1950s a couple of brand-identification experiments were done that pointed in the same direction: people didn't do much better than chance in identifying different brands of American cigarettes when the brand names were obscured, though, in one experiment, they did somewhat better at identifying their own brand.

More recently, Adam Jaffe and Alan Glaros conducted an experiment which found that certain pairs of cigarettes, such as Virginia Slims and Vantage or Vantage and Marlboro Lights, were judged as the same

---

comprehensive list that the Office maintains is tightly controlled, under the stipulations of the 1984 congressional act. (Not even a Freedom of Information Act request from me could pry loose the *number* of additives on the list.)

OSH has set about determining whether any of the substances on its list might be harmful to the public. The Office is authorized to turn over any of its findings to Congress, which would be responsible for taking any action, since, as OSH's Director, Dr. Ronald Davis, notes, "We have no regulatory authority, and neither does anyone else."[16]

The whole question of additives seems to work up the public in a way that is almost comical, however. Tobacco is perfectly capable of killing people in several ways without having anything added to it. It's reasonable to worry whether some *additional* deadly substance will be put into cigarettes, but a person who worries solely about additives is like a person who, while being shot at, worries about whether his assailant is using dumdum bullets.

by close to half of the group of 50 smokers they tested. Only 22 percent of the smokers could correctly identify their own brand from among the seven brands tested.[17] These authors did us the additional service of separating out nicotine content from other factors in the smokers' ability to discriminate among different cigarettes.

They found that smokers *can* distinguish among cigarettes through qualities other than nicotine content (they dubbed the quality they found "sharp-flat"), which seems to settle the issue of whether taste by itself or something like it—the "bite" of the cigarette, for example— *could* play any part in the choices smokers make.

As to how much of a role taste *does* play in smokers' choices, I take the rather poor performances smokers have shown at choosing among brands to be an indication that taste must be fairly loosely related to the choice of brand. Advertising probably plays a big role in decisions made among groupings of cigarettes that are similar in taste.

All this relates to whether smokers choose from among different brands on the basis of taste; it says little about whether taste is a motive *to smoke.* Here, common sense and the little bit of evidence we have indicate that to the degree it's a motive at all, it's a pretty weak one.

Salvatore Zagona and Louis Zurcher, Jr., once surveyed about 1,600 college smokers and found that only about 20 percent said that flavor was a source of enjoyment in smoking for them.[18] A Norwegian survey of a couple of thousand adults, some of them nonsmokers, found that only about 12 percent thought people smoke because of taste.[19] Even these low numbers may be suspect, however. Taste, as we've seen, is one of the few God-fearing reasons for smoking cigarettes, and it may be that people, consciously or not, would attribute more significance to it than is warranted when they're asked about why they smoke.

Finally, we'd be able to take the idea that flavor is a motivator for smoking more seriously if people smoked *anything* on a regular basis that isn't a drug. Think about what people smoke: opium, marijuana, crack cocaine, and tobacco, to name the most popular substances. Every substance I'm aware of that people put into their lungs is, like these compounds, psychoactive. To put this proposition another way: If flavor were much of a motivator in smoking, why, through the centuries, haven't millions of people taken up smoking something whose natural flavor is terrific, rather than something whose flavor needs to be heavily altered, as tobacco's does? My guess is that taste by itself is not a sufficient motive to make people do something that is as inherently goofy as sucking smoke into their lungs.

But tiny increments of reward, added together, move human beings to action, and taste may be one of those increments in smoking. The value of taste as a motivator takes on added significance when we see it as one example of a so-called sensory cue in smoking. Cigarettes provide sensory stimulation in great abundance. Sight, smell, touch, and taste all are stimulated by smoking, and hearing might sneak in the back door if we allow for the wispish sound of burning leaf and the whoosh of exhalation. The human animal naturally seeks sensory stimulation. Psychologists tell us that among other things, such stimulation is "information-giving." It orients us in space and time; it says to us on a continuing basis that our world is here and we are functioning in it.

Of all the stimulations provided by smoking, one type has emerged in recent years as important enough to warrant intensive investigation, and it's with an extended account of it that we will close out this section of our look at smoking motivation.

The stimulation in question is that of the human airway tract, from the mouth through the throat and trachea and into the lungs. The notion of smoking being motivated in part by such upper-airway stimulation has been reported on in scientific journals for decades, but the idea seemed to be going nowhere until it was revived in the mid-1980s by a young researcher named Jed Rose, who heads the Veterans Administration Nicotine Research Laboratory in Durham, North Carolina.

Rose's central idea is straightforward: the satisfaction that smokers derive from cigarettes comes in part from a constellation of physical sensations that are produced by cigarette smoke as it passes through the airway tract. Taste is one of these sensations. Another, more notable sensation, however, is the impact the tiny smoke particles make as they lodge against the back of the throat, the windpipe, and the lungs. This sensation has been described as the "scratch" effect and can be thought of as a kind of rewarding irritation. (In earlier smoking literature, this phenomenon was sometimes referred to as "pulmonary eroticism," which may be the only elegant phrase smoking researchers have ever coined.)

Rose has developed an extended analogy between eating and smoking that serves to illustrate his theory. Scientists have observed that people in experiments who get nutrients intravenously lose only a little of their hunger, even though they may be getting a fair amount of nutrition this way. Likewise, smokers who receive nicotine in the form of, say, nicotine gum, report time and time again that they still have a craving for cigarettes.

"During cigarette smoking, the flavor of cigarette smoke and the throat impact accompanying each puff produce immediate satisfaction," Rose has written, "just as tasting and swallowing food, and the subsequent feeling of fullness in the stomach produce satisfaction when eating."[20] No one would be satisfied by sitting at a dinner table and hooking up to a bottle of glucose, the argument goes; why should we expect smokers to be satisfied by chewing nicotine gum?

To demonstrate that people get something out of upper-airway stimulation, Rose and his colleagues first had to separate the satisfaction it provides from the satisfaction provided by nicotine. They set about doing this by having experimental subjects gargle and inhale a mist containing the anesthetic lidocaine—so that their mouths and airway tracts were numbed—after which they inhaled controlled doses of cigarette smoke. On another occasion, this group of people went through this procedure again, only this time they gargled, and so on, with a saline solution with no anesthetic effect. Before and after each block of puffs, these people were asked how much they craved a cigarette.

The results were that people reported craving a cigarette significantly more in the experiment in which their airways had been numbed. Since the people got the same amount of nicotine into their systems in both experiments, why should this be so? The only difference in the two tests was that in one they couldn't feel the smoke particles and in the other they could.

As it turns out, however, when Rose let these people smoke as they pleased 30 minutes following the controlled smoking, they didn't smoke any more after the numbed condition than after the saline condition, and they had no more craving after one condition than after the other.

What Rose concluded from this is that the *immediate* satisfaction people get from smoking a cigarette may come in part from stimulation of the airway tract by the smoke. The *long-term* satisfaction from smoking, however, may well be dependent on something else, with nicotine being far and away the most likely candidate. Again, he uses a food analogy. When people are dehydrated, they get thirsty and drink liquids. Doing this stimulates nerves leading to the brain that immediately signal, "water level OK now," and thirst ends. This satiation occurs, however, long before the water has reached the sites that originally signaled dehydration. Likewise, Rose thinks, airway stimulation may, at a minimum, signal to the brain, "nicotine level OK now."

Under this argument, airway stimulation draws its strength from being *paired* with nicotine. In psychological terms, it is a conditional reinforcer, and nicotine is an unconditional reinforcer.

This bears an analogy with Pavlov and his famous dog. Meat was an unconditional stimulus for the dog—it made him salivate without being paired with anything. Pavlov's bell was a conditional stimulus: he paired it with the meat, ringing it each time just before the feeding, and eventually it came to stimulate salivation all by itself. This has relevance for the place Rose next takes his argument. After a time, he says, airway stimulation may become rewarding in its own right—it becomes an unconditional reinforcer.

By itself, this doesn't seem very convincing to me. What is there that's *intrinsically* rewarding about tobacco particles smacking into one's windpipe? On the face of it, it doesn't sound much more reward-ing than, say, touching a cool glass—it's something you don't mind doing, but it's probably not pleasurable enough to make you want to do it again. As it turns out, though, it seems that cigarettes provide a direct *nicotine* reward through airway stimulation. If we ask why inhaling tobacco smoke should be an unconditional reinforcer, this, I believe, is a much more likely candidate.

Karl Ginzel is a pharmacologist at the University of Arkansas who has been working with nicotine for better than 20 years. He has per-formed experiments with cats in which he has injected nicotine into a chamber of their hearts, the right atrium, that contains blood that is bound for the lungs. Upon getting these injections, two things hap-pened to the cats: their muscles relaxed and they became more alert.[21] (They were, in fact, awakened from sleep into a state of mild arousal.)

In and of itself, this effect is not particularly surprising; as we'll see later, nicotine is capable of all kinds of dual actions of this sort.

The remarkable thing that Ginzel and his colleagues have found is that these reactions take place one to two seconds after the nicotine has been injected. This is not a sufficient amount of time for the nicotine to go though the bloodstream and reach the brain and the peripheral organs. The effects in the cat begin even before the nicotine is pumped into general circulation. What's happening?

Ginzel has found that these effects are transmitted by nerve fibers located *in the lungs*. Sensory nerve endings there respond to nicotine and transmit messages directly to the brain. What's more, these lung fibers can be stimulated by the nicotine in cigarette smoke as easily as by nicotine from atrial injections. In other words, the circulatory system isn't needed to get nicotine's effects rolling: airway stimulation will do the trick.

One of the arguments against airway stimulation as a motive for smoking is that millions of people use tobacco in forms that offer no throat scratch at all. In fact, cigarettes are the only form that does provide this stimulation. Chewing and snuffing obviously offer none, and pipe and cigar smokers rarely inhale; such airway stimulation as these smokers get would have to be limited to the mouth—leaving out Ginzel's nerve fibers entirely. But, in the America of the 19th century, chewing reigned supreme; in the gentrified England of the 18th century, it was snuff. The tobacco habit was passed down for generations in these environments without anyone getting a bit of pulmonary eroticism.

It seems to me, however, that an argument *for* airway stimulation—combining the reasoning of Rose and Ginzel—can be made along these same kinds of historical lines. Why is it that cigarettes accounted for 2 percent of the tobacco market 100 years ago but now account for 95 percent? Plenty of speculation exists on this topic. There are, for example, sociological theories put forward, such as that cigarettes are a "quick smoke" suited to a stopwatch society.

The mass movement to cigarettes is also consistent, however, with the airway reward that cigarettes—and only cigarettes—provide. The fact that people use tobacco in other forms merely demonstrates that airway stimulation isn't the *only* reason people ingest tobacco.

This argument about the direct effects of inhaling can be carried further, to a discussion of other drugs, where the historical record is just as provocative. Morphine's natural source, opium, was by and large a recreational or therapeutic drug in China prior to the time people began *smoking* it. Only then, beginning in the 18th century, did ravaging addiction become widespread throughout the Chinese populace.* In this regard, it's worth noting that a researcher named Hreday Sapru has demonstrated that the nerve endings in the lungs that respond to nicotine also contain receptors for morphine.[22]

Closer to our own experience, cocaine was a serious problem in the United States throughout the 1970s and early 1980s, but it exploded as a crisis in the mid-1980s when a smokable form of the drug, crack, became widely available.

A postulate in drug research is that the faster a drug acts, the more rewarding it is; quite apart from the arguments Rose and Ginzel make, it's clear that drugs get into circulation faster when they're smoked than when they're swallowed or snorted. The notion that Rose and Ginzel add, however, is that—for tobacco, at least—its inhaled form may be more addictive not just because it works faster, but because it provides *additional* effects for the users almost instantaneously. The parallels with other drugs are obvious, but also obviously speculative.

It's too early to tell how this will come out, but my feeling is that airway stimulation may turn out to be an important part of the cigarette smoking puzzle. Right now, that puzzle has a big piece missing: Why do people still desire cigarettes even when they're given nicotine through other routes? The theory of airway stimulation aims its sights right at this question of "craving." After getting one result after another that served to confirm his ideas, Rose has moved on to apply this work to two practical goals: devising new ways to help people quit smoking and developing a "safer" cigarette (which has been something of a Holy

---

*We have good reason to believe that smoking, as a concept, came to the Chinese by way of tobacco smoking and that the concept was then applied in the 18th century to the smoking of opium, which until then had only been taken orally. If so, given what happened to the Chinese populace, we have in tobacco a spectacular example of a "gateway" drug, or at least a gateway technique.[23]

Grail in smoking research for decades). Time will tell what lies in store for the whole area.

Readers may have noted that, although this chapter is supposedly dedicated to the reasons people smoke *apart* from the effects of nicotine, we have dealt with nicotine extensively. As smoking baffles smokers, so does it baffle writers trying to parse out its effects into neat, separate categories. We will now, however, *really, really* move on into nicotine proper. As a kind of auguring of what is to come, however, think back to the two effects of nicotine that Karl Ginzel found when he injected his sleeping cats: physical relaxation and mental stimulation. What a delicious sounding combination. What a paradox. What a drug.

CHAPTER 3

Stimulating People, Putting Elephants to Sleep

Q<small>UESTIONS ABOUT DRUG</small> abuse have been with civilization at least since antiquity—Roman society was aware that it had a problem with alcohol—but the toughest drug questions have remained with us from that time to this. How can people be weaned permanently from addictive substances? How can we know who will be able to take such substances in moderation and who will fall into the maw of compulsion? Progress has been made in both these areas but, barring some scientific breakthrough, we will have to wait for the 21st century (at least) before we get definitive answers to these questions. That we are unlikely to come up with answers soon is a measure not of the weakness of science, but rather of the difficulty of the problem.

Drug abuse has to do essentially with human motivation, and it may be that there is no subject as complex as that. The functioning of, say, distant stars is a complex thing, but the laws of physics present a formidable set of restrictions as to how stars *might* work. Physicists are much aided by the knowledge that in the physical systems they study, most things that are not forbidden are compulsory. Hence astrophysicists can work on stars by applying mathematics to observation. Where are our equations for human motivation? There aren't any, of course, because the variables are too many, and the knowledge we have too limited.

A case could be made that human motivation has no equal in terms of complexity on the grounds that the most complex object we know of— short of people themselves—is the human brain, which sits atop human motivation, both literally and figuratively, but does not comprise the whole, since cultural and environmental factors also play a part.

If science has not yet had much success with human motivation as it relates to substance abuse, it has done better with understanding abused substances themselves. By the 19th century, chemistry had progressed far enough that scientists were able to pinpoint the specific compounds that put the bang in naturally occurring plants. Morphine was isolated—that is, separated out—from opium poppies in 1803 by Friedrich Wilhelm Serturner.[1] Cocaine was isolated from the coca leaf by Albert Niemann in 1859–1860[2] and nicotine was isolated from tobacco by Posselt and Reimann in 1828.[3]

When we compare these drugs, we notice that nicotine differs from the other two in that it never hit the big time in society as an isolated drug, whereas morphine and cocaine did. Once pure morphine and cocaine were available, they began to be used extensively by the populace at large. This was partly because both drugs had significant medical uses, morphine as a painkiller and cocaine as a local anesthetic. But both became drugs of abuse as well, morphine beginning early in the 19th century and cocaine toward century's end. They were available not only in pure form, but as ingredients in everything from cough syrups to Coca-Cola. This never happened with nicotine; no one ever made up a Dr. Brown's Tonic containing a jolt of nicotine. Only recently have corporations moved to make nicotine available in forms isolated from tobacco—in aerosols, for example—and these products seem to be aimed at people who can't quit smoking.

It's tempting to speculate that nicotine was never produced in products separate from tobacco goods for the simple reason that people have little use for nicotine except when it comes bound up in leaf or plug. The pharmaceutical entrepreneurs of the 19th century—legally as free to dispense morphine as aspirin—were extremely adept at giving the buying public whatever it wanted in the way of drugs and related paraphernalia. In its 1897 mail order catalogue, Sears Roebuck offered a selection of hypodermic syringe kits.[4] If industry didn't deliver a range of nicotine products as it did for morphine and cocaine, the reason may well have been that such products weren't desirable.

This may simply be another way of saying that nicotine's best delivery apparatus is the cigar or the cigarette, whereas for morphine or heroin the apparatus of choice is the hypodermic needle. We have seen already how efficient inhaled cigarette smoke can be at getting the effects of nicotine going from lung to brain. Consider its general circulatory effects. When a person inhales cigarette smoke, the nicotine it carries reaches the brain, via the bloodstream, in about 8 seconds, which is less time than it would take to get there had the person injected it intravenously.[5] By the time 15 to 20 seconds have elapsed, nicotine has made it to the body's last outpost, the big toe.[6]

As a delivery system, inhalation is more efficient than any Dr. Brown's Nicotine Tonic that might be developed; such a tonic would be largely inactivated in the stomach and the liver before it passed into general circulation. By contrast, more than 90 percent of the nicotine in inhaled cigarette smoke is absorbed by the lung.[7]

It is a good thing that so much of the nicotine that is swallowed becomes inactivated; were this not the case, young children who eat cigarettes might suffer more than just the vomiting, convulsions, and diarrhea that they do get.[8] Nicotine is a powerful drug and a little goes a long way. "Capture guns" used to take wild animals alive once employed nicotine darts to bring down creatures as big as elephants.[9] A person who drinks a five-ounce cup of coffee ingests about 120 milligrams of caffeine. A person who ingested half that much nicotine would probably die as a result.[10] Smokers get what they need from the *one* milligram of nicotine that is delivered, on average, in each cigarette.[11]

This is barely a large enough quantity to be seen, even if a whole cigarette's dosage were concentrated into a single drop. As it happens, though, nicotine enters the body in the form of thousands of little droplets, each suspended in a solid particle of partially burned tobacco (which is what "tar" is). These nicotine droplets are so small that they can penetrate into the tiniest branches of the lungs. There they are picked up, hitchhiker-like, by blood that has been sent to the lungs to take up oxygen. From the lungs, it's a fast trip to the left side of the heart, where nicotine is pumped out to every corner of the body.

Scientists sometimes speak of a "cascade" of effects stemming from one cause. This term surely is appropriate in the case of nicotine. From the instant it hits the lungs, its effects come spilling out this way and that, only to loop back on each other and start whole new processes rolling. Scientific sensors aren't required to know that some of these effects are taking place. With the first cigarette of the day, heart rate will increase by 10 to 20 beats per minute. Blood pressure will go up 5 to 10 points.[12] Body temperature will drop in the fingertips as the blood vessels there are constricted.

These effects don't increase by this much *more* with each cigarette smoked. (Alas: if they did, nobody would smoke cigarettes.) But, given the length of time nicotine persists in the bloodstream, an average smoker will go around all day and all night in an altered state. The level of nicotine in the bloodstream increases throughout the day in a way that bears a seafaring analogy. Waves of nicotine come with each cigarette and quickly pass, but the tide of nicotine climbs gradually through the day and then falls during sleep. The tide is high enough and its fall gradual enough, however, that for most smokers, nicotine is active in them 24 hours a day. They are never off the drug.

Where does nicotine get its power? How does it make for fast hearts and devoted smokers? The general answer is the nervous system. So unmistakable are its effects there that, before it was scrutinized as an addictive drug, nicotine was used to "map" a good part of the human nervous system.[13] In fact, it was work on nicotine's effects that led scientists at the turn of the century to postulate that chemicals are involved in transmitting messages between nerve cells.[14] But here we've gotten slightly ahead of ourselves. This kind of chemical transmission may be a little mysterious to most people, and it's important to our story, so let's take a moment to examine it.

Each time you turn a page of this book, a message that tells your hand to move must go out from an area near the top of your brain called the *motor cortex,* then down through the brain stem and spinal cord and out to the hand. (If you're turning the pages with your right hand, it goes from the top *left side* of your brain.) In terms of the distance covered from brain to hand, most of this transmission is electrical (or, more exactly, electrochemical). This transmission doesn't involve exactly the same kind of electricity that runs between a wall socket and a waffle iron—among other things the nervous system transmission is slower—but it is similar. When a single nerve cell (called a *neuron*) fires, it sends an electrical message down a nerve fiber extending from it that is called an *axon.*

Our message from brain to hand has a long way to go, however, and its path will be more complex than that from one cell through one axon. On its way from the motor cortex, it will go through numerous other nerve cells. But: axons only carry messages *away from* nerve cells, and these axonic cables go only so far before they come to an end. For our message to be transmitted to other neurons down the line, it must be picked up by nerve fibers called *dendrites,* which can transmit messages *to* these downstream neurons.

Axons and dendrites do not make up an unbroken electrical line, however, because they do not touch one another. They come close— within about 20 billionths of a meter—but they are separated by a tiny gap. This gap is usually called the *synaptic cleft,* for the reason that the entire junction of axon and dendrite is called a *synapse.*

How does our electrical message make it through the gap? It is transformed into a *chemical* message for its journey across the cleft. When the electrical signal hits the end of an axon, the axon's vesicles secrete a substance they have stored, called a *neurotransmitter,* which flows out into the synaptic cleft. When the neurotransmitter reaches the end point of the dendrite—on the other side of the gap—it joins with a chemical on the surface of the dendrite, called a *receptor.* When neurotransmitter and receptor have bound together, the resulting combination stimulates the dendrite to transmit a new *electrical* signal down the line to the next nerve cell or to another dendrite, and the process continues. In brief, this is a process that goes: electrical, chemical, electrical.

Now, the nervous system is able to achieve its spectacular versatility because there are dozens of these neurotransmitters, and they work *selectively* on dendritic receptors. In other words, not every receptor site will respond to every transmitter. Think of a neurotransmitter as a man who has come to a 1920s speakeasy to deliver a message. He knocks at the door, the peephole opens, and he says, "Louie sent me." This is the message the bouncer is taught to respond to, so he opens the door and our man moves in. If, however, he tells the bouncer, "*Harry* sent me," he gets nowhere. Door stays shut, message is not delivered.

One of the body's most important neurotransmitters is called *acetylcholine* (ACH). It works at the synaptic junctions where nerves and muscles meet (in the hand, for example); it is very important in the body's autonomic nervous system, which controls involuntary bodily functions such as heart rate; and it works within the brain itself, helping send messages from one part to another. Now, as it turns out, nicotine can mimic the effects of acetylcholine. In an array of areas where ACH will work as a neurotransmitter, nicotine will work in its stead. Recall that our discussion of nicotine's effects started with the observation that at the turn of the century, nicotine was used to "map" parts of the nervous system. Nicotine was applied to nerve tissue, and scientists followed its effects through the neural circuitry; receptors that responded to nicotine just as they would to acetylcholine were dubbed *nicotinic* receptors, which is what scientists call them to this day.

As we've observed, ACH works throughout the body; we now see that this is another way of saying that nicotine works throughout the body—it works wherever there are nicotinic receptors. One of its most important effects at these receptor sites is that it can stimulate the release of *other* neurotransmitters. For example, our adrenal glands, which sit on top of our kidneys, have nicotinic receptors on them, and when they get a dose of nicotine (or ACH) they release the neurotransmitters *norepinephrine* and *epinephrine,* the latter of which is better known as *adrenaline.* It is these neurotransmitters that are responsible for some of the stimulating effects of nicotine. Likewise, the increased blood pressure that results from the first cigarette of the day comes about because blood vessels themselves release norepinephrine when the nicotine comes in contact with them.

Note that these are stimulant responses to a drug. This is just what you would expect with a drug that stimulates the adrenal glands, because these are the organs of the classic human fight-or-flight response. What happens if we are actually threatened with getting a punch in the mouth? Our bodies know what we need for a possible fight or flight and they adjust without our thinking about it: plenty of blood at the heart for increased output, increased heart rate for the same reason, and less blood going to our extremities for the simple reason that we need the blood at our body's core. Push liquid through a narrow hole—partially cover the nozzle of a garden hose with your thumb, for instance—and what do you get? Increased pressure; what we get here is increased *blood* pressure when blood vessels on the periphery are narrowed.

Epinephrine and norepinephrine do all these things once they are released into our system. And they do it whether they are released because of a physical threat—which sends ACH to the adrenal glands and blood vessels—or because of the inhalation of cigarette smoke, which sends nicotine to them.

This is not to say that this kind of stimulation is *all* that nicotine does; as we will see, it's busy throughout the body in a lot of different ways. But these effects are a good example of how nicotine works as a neurotransmitter and a stimulant. (By the way, its effects in this regard are very similar to those of cocaine and amphetamines; both of them kick in the adrenal glands as well.)

Having observed these stimulant effects, though, recall that when people are asked why they smoke, they most often reply that they do so because it relaxes them. Recall, too, that at one time nicotine was used to make elephants *very* relaxed—it sedated them into unconsciousness. How can these effects take place with a drug that seems to be such a stimulant?

For our answer—or part of it, at least—we have to look once again at that important space, the synaptic cleft. As we've seen, nervous system messages make it across the cleft through a kind of chemical ferryboat arrangement: neurotransmitters are secreted into the cleft by vesicles at the end of an axon; they cross the gap to the dendritic receptors and bind with them; this turns the newly formed chemical signal back into an electrical signal for transmission down the line.

Nerve signals, however, come continuously. It's not as if a given synapse transmits a message and then sits idle for half a minute. Each synapse is connected to a vast network of dendrites and nerve cells.

There are at least 10^{14} synapses in the cortex of a human brain alone—which is one hundred *trillion* synapses.[15] A single neuron in the brain may receive input from tens of thousands of synapses; thus a synapse may be called on to transmit a great many messages very rapidly.

Synapses do not do this by simply staying "on." In some synapses, once a message has been transmitted, the dendrite releases a protein that breaks up the transmitter, after which parts of it are taken back up by the axon terminal to be used again. This is what happens with the transmitter we're most concerned with, acetylcholine. What's important to note is that the synaptic cleft is "cleared" by this process, in less than the blink of an eye, for new transmissions that may be coming.

We've noted that nicotine can serve the function of acetylcholine at many receptor sites. In a sense, however, it's more powerful than ACH, because the bond it makes with the receptor is stronger and longer lasting.[16] In small doses, nicotine will stimulate transmission at nicotinic sites, but in large doses it begins to *impede* transmission by staying bound with the receptor. In this case, the synapse cannot be completely cleared for new transmission. In huge doses, nicotine stops transmission altogether. This is how people can die from a nicotine overdose: their respiratory circuits simply cease to function because messages can't get through. Think of our earlier analogy of the man coming to the speakeasy to deliver a message. Large doses of nicotine are like a very *fat man* coming to the door. He knows the password the bouncer wants to hear. Having said it, and having been granted admission, however, he is so fat that he blocks the door so that no one else can get through.

So nicotine can work in two ways. In the argot of the scientist, its effects are *biphasic*. A little stimulates, a lot sedates. Actually, however, we should put this in a slightly different way: a little nicotine stimulates and a lot sedates *in laboratory settings*—that is, in experimental settings in which pharmacologists are able to apply large doses of nicotine to isolated pieces of nerve tissue. Does it work this way, however, in the most unclinical of settings: in a nervous smoker taking big drags off a cigarette? Some smoking researchers have their doubts. Do cigarettes provide enough nicotine to block nicotinic transmission? If nicotine can sedate at the cellular level, does it also work this way in a whole complex human being?

Opinions are divided, but my sense is that a growing body of research indicates that it does. As we'll see, biphasic effects of nicotine have now been documented in a number of areas, prominent among them brain-wave states that are indicative of the level of alertness or arousal in each of us.

Regardless of how this argument comes out, however, the actions of nicotine down among the synapses form an underpinning that we will find useful as we look at the drug's effects on whole human beings, rather than the cells they are made of.

CHAPTER 4

Staying on an Even Keel

Because cigarette ads are ubiquitous in the United States, Americans quite frequently have the opportunity to view what might be called the skull beneath the skin: of taking in the beautiful, laughing Virginia Slims woman at the top of an ad and following her shapely figure down to the Surgeon General's foretelling of her future. Youth and beauty side by side with death and disease, one in living color, the other in black and white.

There are four Surgeon General's warnings and they appear, on a rotating basis, on every cigarette ad and package distributed in the United States. The language in the warnings leaves something to be desired, which is what you might expect given that the wording was arrived at only through a hard-fought set of negotiations with the tobacco lobby. One of the messages lays smoking's health effects right on the line—"Smoking Causes Lung Cancer, Heart Disease, Emphysema, and May Complicate Pregnancy"—but earlier congressional drafts of it added something else: that smoking is addictive.

The other three warnings are less sobering even about health effects. In fact, one of them—"Cigarette Smoke Contains Carbon Monoxide"—seems less a warning than a piece of information the government thought smokers might find handy.

Carbon monoxide (CO) has a considerable reputation for danger, stemming, I would think, from its role as a suicide gas in closed garages. But from the Surgeon General's warning, it's unclear what it does in the amounts that cigarettes provide. One answer to this question is that it may contribute to heart disease. But it also plays a role in the way that smokers process the air they breathe.

Oxygen is carried to the various parts of the body by hemoglobin, a protein in the red blood cells. As oxygen enters the bloodstream from the lungs, it binds with hemoglobin in a process analogous to two people holding on to one another for the duration of a dance. When the hemoglobin reaches its destination, the dance is over; the oxygen splits off to be used within cells, and the hemoglobin returns to the lungs to pick up another partner.

That partner, however, can just as easily be carbon monoxide as oxygen. In fact, hemoglobin binds much more readily with carbon monoxide than with oxygen. The hemoglobin that binds with CO is unavailable to carry oxygen, and there are only so many hemoglobin molecules in the body at any given time. This, then, is one of the reasons that you are unlikely to see any smokers winning the Boston Marathon. It's not just that their lungs are clogged from the effects of tar and hence are inefficient—although that's bound to be true if they've been smoking long enough—it's that a fair number of their hemoglobin molecules are engaged in carrying poison rather than life-sustaining oxygen. (The body tries to respond to this chronic condition by creating more red blood cells, but the compensation is incomplete.) People who lock themselves in garages with their motors running are simply carrying out this process on a grand scale. When enough of their hemoglobin is unavailable to carry oxygen, they die.

When carbon monoxide binds with hemoglobin, the result is a molecule called carboxyhemoglobin (COHb), and its level in the bloodstream is a pretty good way to judge a person's actual intake of cigarette smoke products.

In the early 1970s, two British researchers, T. W. Meade and N. J. Wald, decided that it was important to know when people smoked during the day in order to know when to measure them for COHb. If people smoked little during the morning relative to the rest of the day, for example, a morning sampling of COHb would be misleading as to their intake of smoke products. Since the more of these products people take in, the more prone they are in general to disease, COHb levels might serve as a kind of risk marker, the researchers felt.[1] Consequently, Meade and Wald sent a questionnaire to about 3,600 British workers—in factories and offices—asking them when they smoked from the time they got up till the time they went to bed.

This research subsequently has been cited not so much in connection with COHb levels, but for what it uncovered about when people smoke. What Meade and Wald found was that those workers not restricted from smoking on the job smoked more than half (56 percent) of their cigarettes daily while at work. Furthermore, the two highest hourly rates of smoking for these people took place in the afternoon while they were at work.

This may not seem so surprising until we begin to think of the kinds of activities we normally associate with psychoactive drugs. The most popular of these substances are generally used for *pleasure,* not for work. What percentage of alcohol use goes on in the workplace? Of marijuana use? Of cocaine use? People do use these drugs at work—cocaine, in particular, is reported to be used to some extent on the job—but in the main their use is recreational. Closer workplace counterparts to tobacco, I think, would be such drugs as Valium or caffeine, taken by workers to keep their skills sharp or, more precisely, to keep their skills from *deteriorating* on the job because of such things as lack of sleep, an overwrought nervous system, or the simple vicissitudes of a working day.

The workplace use of such drugs as Valium or caffeine stands our common notion of drug use on its head. Both these drugs can be used to get "high," as that term is commonly understood, but I would submit that they are most often taken not for the purpose of getting high, but for the purpose of getting normal.[2] What they are doing to make people feel normal is a matter of some debate, as we will see, but a state coming close to what we might call psychological neutrality is, I believe, their primary purpose. There probably is an element of euphoria-seeking in this—my guess is that people want to be just barely to the *high* side of neutral—but the stronger motivation, I believe, is *dysphoria*-avoidance. Thus, these drugs are taken by people who are having trouble concentrating, who are depressed into inactivity, who are jagged from anxiety.

The nicotine in tobacco has many uses. But when we begin to ask why it qualifies as humanity's all-time addictive drug of choice,* one of the first things we might consider is the idea that it can rescue people from several *different* dysphoric states, returning them to normal from several locations on the psychological map. This is exactly what we would expect of a drug that is heavily used in the workplace, where normal is what's called for and where the forces pulling people away from that state range from boredom to stress.

In the late 1960s, Norman Heimstra and his colleagues at the University of South Dakota conducted a series of experiments that were aimed at seeing how smoking affected the performance of various tasks, such as simulated driving, in which subjects tracked a moving target. Before and after these tasks were carried out, however, Heimstra's subjects filled out a standardized psychological questionnaire that asked them to rate their mood along several lines. How aggressive did they feel? How talkative? How fatigued?

In the first of these experiments, Heimstra had 60 subjects perform the driving task for *six hours* without a pause. Twenty of these people were nonsmokers, 20 were smokers allowed to smoke, and 20 were smokers prohibited from smoking. Not much of interest was turned up in terms of performance differences among these groups, but when Heimstra looked at the *mood* results, he found something intriguing. In the case of the nonsmokers, their mood changed significantly in five areas over the course of the driving task: their aggression increased, as did their fatigue; meanwhile, their social warmth decreased, along with

---

*The operative word here is *addictive*. Caffeine is almost surely the world's most popular drug, but it seems to flunk at least one of the standard tests for *addictive* drugs: animals don't care for it in laboratory settings.[3]

their concentration and their "surgency," defined as the degree to which they were in a playful, talkative state.

The smokers who smoked, however, had significant mood changes in only two areas: like the nonsmokers, they had less concentration and more fatigue after the driving task than before it. But their reported level of aggression did not rise. Likewise, their surgency and their social affection remained unchanged.[4]

Heimstra and his colleagues ran four more experiments that were similar to this—in one, the subjects watched a film on the bombing of Hiroshima and Nagasaki—and the results were much the same in all of them: nonsmokers had much greater fluctuations in their mood states than did smokers who smoked over the course of one of these trying experiences.

In 1984, D. R. Cherek of the LSU Medical Center in Shreveport, Louisiana, conducted an experiment that lent support to Heimstra's findings in one particular mood dimension: aggression. He recruited half a dozen subjects, all smokers, under the pretense that he was looking into the effects of cigarettes on reaction time and information processing. What he was actually investigating was the effects of smoking on aggression, but he couldn't tell these people that, lest this information taint the results.[5]

These smokers were told that they would be paired with another person, hidden from them in a remote location, who would play a kind of electronic game with them. There actually was no such person—just the researchers manipulating the contest in a way that made it appear there was. The subjects were seated at a console that presented them with a couple of buttons, a switch, and a numerical counter. By pressing button A, they got to accumulate money—at 10 cents per 100 presses—and the counter displayed a running total of their accumulations, which they got to keep at the end of their sessions.

The other button and the switch were ostensibly wired to their fellow player at a similar console. By pressing button B 10 times, they were told, they could *subtract* 10 cents from the total of the other player; 10 hits on switch C, meanwhile, would deliver a blast of white noise to the other player from a speaker placed over his console. This other player supposedly had this same setup: he could accumulate money, subtract money from the first player, or give *him* a blast of white noise.

Cherek had his subjects come in five days a week, 30 minutes before the test began and had them (*a*) not smoke, (*b*) smoke experimental low-nicotine cigarettes, or (*c*) smoke experimental high-nicotine cigarettes.

He knew from preliminary studies of this research method that people didn't like being hit with a blast of white noise, but that they perceived having money taken away from them as a much more aggressive and annoying action. (I take this as a profound comment on human values: people will accept being hit in the face with a high-decibel insult, but taking their money is serious business.)

The results of this experiment were that the more nicotine these people had in their systems, the less aggressively they acted toward their fellow "players." The subtract-money response was decreased in all subjects when they smoked the low-nicotine cigarettes and was decreased even further when they smoked the high-nicotine brand. The white-noise responses followed the same pattern, but weren't as uniform. One way of looking at this is that the more aggressive option—subtracting money—was affected more by nicotine. Interestingly, both the high and the low doses of nicotine *increased* the number of add-money responses per session. Cherek concludes from this that the suppressive effects of nicotine on aggression were not due to a "generalized depression action." What was indicated instead, he said, was a more specific, selective action of the drug.

When we ask how nicotine might be able to reduce aggression, some provocative evidence has been provided by Ronald Hutchinson and Grace Emley, who, in the early 1970s, did some work with nicotine and animals and then set about applying the results they got to human beings.[6] In the animal trials, they used squirrel monkeys seated in a "restraint chair" with their long tails shaved and attached to electrodes. (Animal lovers may wish to skip the descriptions of these experiments and cut to the results.)

In this stockade condition, the monkeys had several objects within reach: a rubber hose, which they could bring to their mouths, and a response lever or a pull chain, which they could reach with their hands. The hose was used to measure biting attack behavior, which, a raft of earlier experiments had shown, was a reliable sign of aggression or fighting behavior in the monkeys. Among the conditions that can bring on this behavior is electric shock, which in this case meant a 400-volt shock delivered to the animal's shaved tail for a tenth of a second once every four minutes.

When this jolt was received, the biting attack behavior would occur, meaning that the monkey would bite rapidly and repetitively on the rubber hose. Then the biting would fall off until the next shock *approached*. With this, the monkey—knowing what was coming—would start biting the hose more frequently until the last few seconds before the shock was delivered, at which point it quit biting altogether.

What can a restrained monkey do when faced with the certainty that it is going to be hit with a 400-volt shock in, say, 30 seconds? One thing it would like to do is flee, and, as it turns out, the other responses available—pulling on the chain or pressing on the lever—are reliable indications of this escape response. (What would any of us do when trapped and facing pain? My guess is that we would flail about to whatever degree we could, hoping that something would change just by dint of our movement.) The escape response in the monkeys was driven not by the shock, but by the *anticipation* of it: the closer the time for the shock came, the more the monkeys would press the lever or pull the chain until just before shock delivery, when—as with the biting response—their movement would stop altogether.

With these responses to "noxious" stimuli established, Hutchinson and Emley set about seeing how different drugs would affect the monkeys' behavior under these conditions. It turned out that amphetamines and caffeine tended to increase both the biting and the lever pressing. By contrast, morphine decreased both activities.

Nicotine, however, did something altogether different. It decreased the attack behavior, but it increased the escape response. In a fascinating twist, the drugs that it was similar to in this regard were not opiates or amphetamines, but tranquilizers. It showed the same pattern as chlordiazepoxide, for example, which is better known by its trade name, Librium.

Ultimately, Hutchinson and Emley were as much interested in people as in monkeys, and they devised experiments to see if they could extend their monkey results to human beings. What the researchers measured this time was not biting, but human jaw clenching, which they had found to be a reliable indicator of irritability and aggressiveness in human beings. They hooked electrodes to the massiter and temporalis muscles of their subjects (on the jaw and temple) and counted the jaw-clenching muscle contractions that ensued under various conditions. (Finding out about this made me wonder if jaw clenching is simply what remains of the biting response once it has been softened by civilization.)

The noxious stimulus in one experiment was not a 400-volt electric shock but a 110-decibel blast of noise; in another experiment, the researchers measured the jaw clenching of people who had recently quit smoking.

In the stop-smoking experiment, seven of their eight subjects increased their spontaneous jaw clenching upon quitting, with the biggest jump in responses coming generally in the first week after quitting and then dropping off thereafter.

The noise experiment was carried out with nonsmokers who were hit with a 3,000-hertz tone for 2 seconds every 3 minutes. The subjects drank 5 ounces of water each day, 15 minutes prior to testing, to which the researchers eventually added a small amount of nicotine. The results were that all these people had reduced jaw-clenching responses on the days that they got nicotine.

We've looked in some detail now at three sets of experiments that all point in the same general direction: nicotine *moderates* mood shifts that are brought about by stressful influences. It seems to diminish aggression, while helping people to maintain sociability and an even tone. Just as important, it does these things without having a generalized numbing effect. Heimstra's smoking drivers performed just as well as nonsmokers; Cherek's game-players acted in their own self-interest (accumulating money); and Emley and Hutchinson's monkeys worked assiduously to flee from the shock.

My own feeling about these results is that they bear some rough comparison with the effects K. H. Ginzel found when he injected cats with nicotine (relaxed muscles, alert minds). The specific effects he found are separate from these, of course, but *multiple,* somewhat dissimilar effects are common to all the experiments.

Assuming that effects like these do take place in smokers, the real question that presents itself is: Who wouldn't want to have this kind of emotional fine-tuning at his or her disposal? Recall that this whole discussion started with the assertion that, to a large extent, tobacco is a *work* drug. The effects we've seen evidence of make tobacco seem like a good candidate for an advertisement that goes: "Lose the aggression, keep the ability; smoke tobacco."*

We've also noted, however, that another worker's enemy is lack of stimulation—in a word, boredom. If the forces we've looked at so far—aggression, fear, anger—have a strong emotional content to them, boredom, it seems to me, is much more a purely mental condition. (If you like, it involves a *lack* of emotion.) Can tobacco do anything to influence this drowsy state of affairs? The short answer is yes.

---

*In the preface, I noted that I would not be going into an exhaustive set of arguments for and against these kinds of claims; rather, I would summarize the case *for* effects that, to my way of thinking, have an impressive amount of evidence supporting them.

Skeptical readers may therefore have wondered what they're missing. Let's use just this one effect we've been talking about as an example of what I've left out. The evidence I've presented for the tranquilizing effects of tobacco is consistent and, to my way of thinking, convincing. But it's important to realize that we've looked at three sets of experiments out of perhaps dozens that have been conducted on this general topic. If we were to walk through this whole body of work, things wouldn't look so neat and tidy. We'd find some experiments that give no support to the idea that nicotine can act as a tranquilizer, and we'd find scientific reviews that criticized some of the experiments we *have* looked at.

The Cherek experiment is a good example of a scientific test that's open to criticism. Recall, first of all, that he had a small number of subjects (six people), which usually counts against you in science. Second, all these people were smokers. By the time they'd finished with their add-money, subtract-money test, the "deprived" smokers among them had not had a cigarette for 90 minutes. So, did *getting* the nicotine tranquilize these people or did *not* having it put them in a state of nicotine withdrawal, which made them more aggressive?

This is a constantly recurring conundrum in smoking research. You might think it could be solved just by including nonsmokers in all such experiments, but things aren't that easy. Suppose Cherek had recruited some nonsmokers. How does he give them the nicotine? Do they smoke, in which case they'd probably get nauseous as most first-time smokers do? If they got it through an IV, nausea still would be a problem, and their play probably would have been affected by having a tube sticking out of their arms. We know that it's difficult to mimic the effects of smoking by giving someone a nicotine tablet.

The other two experiments we looked at aren't so much subject to this kind of criticism (which is one reason I selected them), but the notion of smoking affecting mood in the way I've suggested does have its critics. The Surgeon General's report on nicotine somewhat grudgingly conceded that the evidence on nicotine and mood generally supports the view that nicotine can moderate negative mood states in animals; however, as to humans, it concluded that the case is not proved, owing to some methodological limitations of the studies conducted.[7] "Truth" here is elusive, perhaps nonexistent. What I'm presenting is evidence that seems to me to be persuasive, but that's of course a far different thing from its being incontrovertible.

CHAPTER 5

Doing Something With It, Doing Without It

EARLIER, WHEN WE looked at the way nicotine functions at the cellular level, we noted that the effects of the first cigarette of the day on the average smoker are likely to resemble the effects of stimulation of the body's sympathetic—that is, fight-or-flight—nervous system. Heart rate goes up, blood vessels are constricted, and so forth. This is clearly a stimulation effect; whether moved to this state by a frightening noise or the smoking of a cigarette, the body in this condition is primed for action.

In general, a similar effect takes place in the brain when a person smokes a cigarette: the brain moves to a state of higher arousal. The time-honored way of measuring this is through brain-wave states. Since nervous system transmission is essentially electrical transmission, it follows that we ought to be able to measure the electrical current flowing in the brain. That's exactly what scientists—and biofeedback enthusiasts—do by placing electrodes on the head to measure the current flowing within. Measured by an electroencephalograph (EEG), this current is simply the sum total of the firing of the individual cells we talked about earlier. The cells can be thought of as snowflakes, if you like, that result in the measurable snow accumulation of the brain-wave states.

The problem with this procedure is that brain-wave states are mere averages of an underlying brain activity of vast complexity and diversity. (I once heard a scientist compare the procedure to trying to find out something about the Chinese people by hanging a single microphone over Beijing.) Even with this limitation, though, EEG readings are still one of our best tools for measuring levels of activity in the brain.

Brain waves measured by EEG are broken down into four categories—delta, theta, alpha, and beta—and these describe a continuum of arousal, from lower to higher. Put electrodes on an average person, have him take a deep breath and close his eyes, and he's likely to go into the alpha state, with the electroencephalograph registering brain waves of about 8 to 14 cycles per second. (This, by the way, is the state that the biofeedback enthusiasts are trying to get people into.) Shine a light on his closed eyes, however, and the alpha waves cease to dominate and are replaced by the faster beta waves, moving at better than 14 cycles per second. Upon lying down to go to sleep, a person may go from this alert beta state, back through the more relaxed alpha state, and then finally, in deepest sleep, into the delta state, with the brain waves coming at only 1 to 4 cycles per second.

There are also different levels of activity *within* these different categories. What's called the *dominant frequency*—again measured in cycles per second—can rise or fall, with a higher dominant frequency indicating greater arousal. In lower alpha states, brain activity tends to come in bursts, with many cells firing at once. As you move up the frequency scale, the cortical activity tends to get more evened out: it becomes *desynchronized,* indicating higher arousal.

Where does nicotine fit in? Since the late 1950s, it has been known that nicotine generally causes EEG arousal in humans and animals.[1] If a person smokes a cigarette, dominant alpha frequency is likely to go up, along with desynchronization. In many of the studies that have shown this, scientists have had to grapple with the old smoking conundrum: Is nicotine stimulating these smokers' brains, or is it bringing them back from a *depressed* cortical state brought on by nicotine withdrawal? Is it, in other words, returning addicted people to a normal state by replenishing their bodies with the addictive drug? One way to get around this question, at least partially, is to give nicotine to non-smokers by, say, intravenous injection. This has been done, and we find much the same thing: nicotine stimulates the brain, as measured by brain-wave states.[2]

All arousals are not created equal, however. Interestingly, in some monkey experiments done in the 1970s, the EEG arousal produced by nicotine was very much like the EEG arousal produced by normal sensory stimulation—by the animals' hearing an arresting sound or seeing an intriguing figure, for example. Conversely, caffeine or amphetamines, while producing the same *level* of stimulation, produced brain-wave patterns that differed significantly from normal arousal.[3]

EEG measurements are taken from the brain's cortex or outer layer, but the primary seat of human arousal is located in another part of the brain entirely. Viewed in diagram from the side, the brain looks kind of like a lopsided head of cauliflower, complete with a stem extending beneath it. Contained within the *brain stem,* beginning at about the place where the neck becomes the head, there is a group of cells called the *reticular formation* that is the most important area in human arousal. The reticular formation sends nerve fiber projections up and out to all areas of the cerebral cortex. Stimulate certain parts of the reticular formation and the brain moves to a state of greater arousal. You don't need drugs or electrodes to achieve this reticular stimulation: getting tapped on the shoulder will suffice; getting a balloon popped behind your back will do it on a grand scale. This is the sensory arousal we talked about earlier; one of the main things the reticular formation does is to act as a kind of hotel clerk, giving a wake-up call to other parts of the brain when this sensory stimulation comes in.

We have good reason to believe that nicotine is achieving much of its alerting effect on the brain by way of its action on the reticular activating system. Recall that cells in the system contain nicotinic receptors that respond to nicotine as well as they would to the body's own neurotransmitter, acetylcholine. Further, nicotine's alerting effects have been blocked in cats when scientists have removed their reticular systems from the neural loop.[4] No reticular formation, no arousal through nicotine.

All of this seems nicely summed up, then, but not for nothing does nicotine have a reputation as "one of the dirtiest drugs in pharmacology," as one scientist expressed it to me. It's not that researchers believe nicotine is hitting below the belt; it's that nicotine does not have nice, clean, *isolated* effects. Its effects instead are all over the place, varying according to dose and individual and sometimes, it may seem, the phase of the moon.

Recall that when smokers are asked why they smoke, the answer they're most likely to give is that it relaxes them. What are we to make of this in light of the fact that smoking increases fight-or-flight reactions and, as we have just seen, stimulates brain activity as well?

One sure answer to this is that at certain times—after the first act of a long play, for example—smoking is "relaxing" smokers by rescuing them from drug withdrawal. This is not much different from what happens with, say, opium addicts; the effects of the drugs are very different, but the underlying syndrome is the same.

We'll look later in more detail at this kind of physical dependence, but for now, let's set it aside and ask whether nicotine could be having any relaxing effects *apart* from its addiction rescue work. (The term "rescue" may seem a bit odd here, but such are the paradoxes in the world of drugs that people are rescued by their jailers.)

The kind of EEG work we talked about before is intriguing here. In animals, large doses of nicotine have shown effects consistent with *sedation,* not stimulation. Larger doses have produced synchronous, slow-wave theta activity, not on the brain's outer layer (the cortex), but in its temporal lobe, in an area called the *hippocampus.* Note how nicely this fits in with the observation we made earlier—using our fat-man-at-the-speakeasy metaphor—about small doses of nicotine stimulating nerve transmission and large doses impeding it.

Such "hippocampal theta" is unknown in human beings, but some research has shown cortical theta being produced in people after smoking—interestingly, in smokers who had type B personalities.[5] Here we get to the syndrome I spoke of just a second ago: the EEG results that researchers get hinge to some degree on who they have doing the smoking and under what conditions. In a series of experiments, researchers G. L. Mangan and J. F. Golding observed subjects in high-arousal situations (giving them a blast of white noise), middle-arousal situations (boredom), and low-arousal situations (a subtle sensory isolation). In general, what they found was that they got depressant effects from nicotine when the subjects got the white noise, mixed effects in the boredom state, and stimulant effects when the subjects were in sensory isolation.[6] Nicotine moved these people in the opposite direction from the environment in which they found themselves.

Scott Lukas of Harvard, who has run IV nicotine experiments, reports watching his subjects repeatedly go through the same sequence of events: the nicotine is delivered, at which point these people sit bolt upright and break out in a sweat, with heart pounding and panic breathing—all for about 30 to 45 seconds. Then this response ends abruptly and they move into a state he saw as a kind of relaxed euphoria.[7]

Now smokers wouldn't put themselves through the first state in order to get to the second, but then, in Lukas's experiments, the subjects weren't doing what smokers normally can do so well: control the dose of nicotine they're getting and the setting they're getting it in.

Our average smoker takes about 200 drags a day, which gives him or her a lot of practice in how to adjust dosage levels. We saw earlier how potent nicotine is at very small dosages (that is, that a little can make a lot of difference). What we begin to see through all this is the ability of smokers to fine-tune their arousal and mood state by taking in *just the right amount* of nicotine in *just the right setting*. We might compare it to an actress making herself up before a stage performance: playing Lady Macbeth, she knows that she needs some base here and then some lipstick; then just a little more liner is needed right here and a touch of blush, and voila! Set up perfectly. Our smoker, by contrast, is mixing his surroundings and dosage levels to set up his *mental* state perfectly. His unconscious is largely doing the directing here. The smoker may not consciously be aware of directions more specific than "more needed" or "level fine," but he is *very* aware of those imperatives.

In smoking research literature, there are what we might call "strong" and "weak" versions of this general argument. The strong version goes something like this. Smoking can *reliably* move people up or down the sedation-stimulation scale according to the dosage of nicotine smokers ingest and the setting in which they ingest it. That is, smaller doses of nicotine stimulate and larger doses sedate. Likewise, in boring situations nicotine is likely to stimulate, while in nerve-wracking ones it is likely to sedate. These two variables are linked in that people often smoke more in jarring situations (to calm themselves) and less in boring ones (to stimulate themselves). Nobody claims that this will *always* be the case, but it will happen more often than not, the argument goes.

The weak case is that smoking can move people in either direction, but not in accordance with a couple of simple variables like this. Body and environment are simply too complex, this view holds, to allow us to make the strong case.

We actually see both parts of the strong case in Mangan and Golding's experiment. Recall that their subjects were sedated by smoking when they were getting the blasts of white noise, but stimulated by smoking when they were placid in sensory isolation. Mangan and Golding also observed, however, that these people took bigger, deeper, and more frequent drags when getting bombarded with the white noise. As scientists would say, this is "consistent" with the notion of larger doses of nicotine being sedating.

One of the most often cited pieces of work consistent with the strong case was done by another team of British researchers, Heather Ashton and her colleagues.[8] They also looked at brain-wave states, but this time not at *resting* states but at a state *evoked* by command. Called the contingent negative variation (CNV), it is a brain wave produced in the brief time between an alerting command ("on your mark") and an action command ("go"). (Is it surprising that there's a unique brain-wave state associated with this short period of time? I think not; it measures a moment that is like no other.) All subjects were in the same starting condition here, but Ashton found that small doses of nicotine stimulated and large doses sedated the CNV response.

Many researchers remain unconvinced by evidence of this sort. The dosages of nicotine aren't properly controlled, they argue, and, in any event, nicotine's effects are much too diverse to be able to say that a little will *predictably* bring you up while a little more will cool you out. Your author professes a safe agnosticism about this whole question. Whichever way the truth lies, however, the more important point is that by controlling dosage and setting, smokers seem to be able to exercise some control over their mental states and to exercise it in directions that we might simply call up and down, for simplicity's sake. This control has to do with alertness, concentration, processing ability, and the like. It is the cognitive side of human beings, which is to put it in opposition to the emotional side we looked at in connection with nicotine's effect on mood and feeling.

We might note that, in terms of performance, being *a little* stimulated will sometimes get us further than being *very* stimulated, depending on what it is we're doing. There is a generally accepted principle in psychology, called the Yerkes-Dodson law, which says that stimulation eventually reaches a point of diminishing returns—it makes us perform worse, in fact—and that the optimal point of stimulation varies according to the task at hand. Our ideal stimulation level is lower for complex tasks, but somewhat higher for simple ones. If, as I've suggested, smoking allows people to move up and down on the sedation-stimulation scale, then the Yerkes-Dodson law would make this fine-tuning ability even more important.

This hypothesis has an implication for what I've only alluded to in passing: The evidence we have indicates that smokers generally use nicotine's control to *moderate* their attentional states. That is, they're not using nicotine to exaggerate their state in one direction or another, but to normalize it: to arouse themselves from boredom or calm themselves from overstimulation. Recall too that, compared to amphetamines or even caffeine, the EEG stimulation provided by nicotine is almost identical to that provided by the environment; it is the stimulation of getting tapped on the shoulder, if you will. People may want to go out and get *high* on amphetamines, they may want to get *low* on Quaaludes, but they seem to want to get *medium* on nicotine. They often seem to be seeking a normality that their environment has taken them out of. This is the opposite of what we commonly think of in terms of "drug use" and is a valuable corrective to an assumption that *altering* our mental states inevitably means getting stoned in one euphoric sense or another.

What we have seen consistently with nicotine thus far is its ability to do many things or, in some cases, its ability to do several different things at once. Ginzel's cats got simultaneously relaxed and alert;

Heimstra's drivers performed well but stayed on an even keel emotionally; Mangan and Golding's smokers varied their attentional states in different ways according to the situation they were in.

Nicotine is not unique in this ability. Other drugs can also have a broad range of effects. Despite its reputation, heroin sometimes prompts its users to start talking their heads off. (Junkies call it "soapboxing.") Marijuana has a reputation for making some people withdraw and others come out. My guess, though, is that though these drugs *can* be used for different purposes, nicotine is something of a champion in the breadth of effects people *do* use it for. If we ask why it has been so wildly popular with the human race, we can now offer a partial answer: because it does a lot of different things for different people. Automobiles are popular for the same reason, while cellos are less so.

If it's true that nicotine has these kinds of cognitive effects, then we ought to be able to detect them when people actually *do* things—when they carry out tasks.

A large amount of experimental work has been done on this topic over the years. (Indeed, up to the 1950s, most of the scientific work on smoking had to do with whether it made people perform better or worse when they were asked to carry out tasks.) Two overarching questions have evolved from this. One of these is now pretty much a closed case, except for filling in a detail here and there: Do smokers who are deprived of nicotine perform worse when asked to do something, such as concentrate for a long time? Not much of a surprise here: the answer is yes.

The second question is: *Apart* from any withdrawal rescue work, can nicotine improve human performance? That is, can it provide true, *absolute* improvements in human functioning? Here we have a wide diversity of scientific opinion, which we'll get to in a minute. For now, though, let's look at the first question in detail.

Anyone who knows a smoker who is trying to quit is likely to hear the complaint that this person "can't think" since he gave up cigarettes. Allowing for hyperbole, this person is right. In fact, he might add that he can't perceive, either.

In the early 1970s, Marianne Frankenhaeuser and her colleagues in Stockholm recruited a group of smokers, had them abstain from smoking overnight, and then put them in an experimental chamber in which they were told to hit a button every time they saw a light go on.[9] The tricky thing was that the light went on at irregular intervals every few seconds and the test continued for 80 minutes. What Frankenhaeuser was measuring was reaction time—how long it took the subjects to hit the button after seeing the light—but the experiment was really a test of sustaining performance over a long period of time in a profoundly boring situation. She had each subject carry out the experiment on two different days: once while refraining from smoking and the other time while smoking controlled doses of tobacco. The results were that, while smoking, the reaction times of these people stayed pretty much the same throughout the 80 minutes. When they did not smoke, however, their reaction times began to slow as the test went on and stayed slower than the smoking-condition times throughout.

Gareth Williams had a group of smokers abstain overnight and then gave them sheets of paper that had printed on them lines of 30 randomly ordered letters.[10] Some of these were the letter *E,* which they were told to cross out as fast as possible over a period of three minutes. The smokers carried out the test after smoking or while continuing abstinence and consistently did dramatically better in the smoking condition.

Verner Knott and Peter Venables had a group of smokers stop smoking for a minimum of 12 hours and then put electrodes on their heads to measure their EEG states.[11] They found that the resting alpha state of these people was depressed compared to a group of nondeprived smokers and a group of nonsmokers: their brain waves were coming more slowly. When the abstainers were allowed to smoke, however, their alpha activity bounced back up. Then, in a separate experiment, Knott and Venables took the same three groups, put them in a darkened room, and subjected them to intermittent flashes of light from a strobe while recording their brain-wave activity. The result was that, compared to smokers and nonsmokers, the abstainers showed a hypersensitivity to the flashes; they experienced the flashes "more readily and more strongly." A normalization of their responses took place when they were allowed to smoke.[12]

I chose these experiments because they involve such different parts of people's cognitive lives: sheer perception with the strobe test; paying attention to something boring with the reaction test; and processing information at a rapid rate with the letter-crossing test. In every case, smoking, or the lack of it, had pronounced effects on the people involved. These task experiments are, of course, simply abstractions of the kinds of things people would be called upon to do in their normal working lives. Given this, if we ask, why do people smoke? one clear and compelling reason is that, for a time at least, they have a great deal of trouble carrying out their day-to-day chores *without* smoking.

How long does this go on? Jack Henningfield and his colleagues at the Addiction Research Center in Baltimore performed a battery of these tests and found clear impairments beginning within 8 hours of the last cigarette smoked and almost no improvement in performance over the next 10 days of abstinence—at which point the experiment was terminated—so the troubles go on at least that long.[13]

A little finer point should be put on this whole question in relation to perception. Recall the flashgun findings of Knott and Venables: deprived smokers experienced the flashes "more readily and more strongly."[14] This has its counterparts in other sensory areas. We have reason to believe, for example, that a *lowered* sensitivity may take place in connection with hearing for deprived smokers. It may well be that things actually look different and sound different to people who are trying to quit smoking. One might say that their world is too much and too little with them. Their brains react more intensely to light, less intensely to sound. People tend to think of perception as one unvarying and undifferentiated whole, as if vision, hearing, and touch were taking in whatever they encounter with the passivity of a camera lens. But our senses are really more like a set of soldiers working together in close-order drill, each susceptible to doing too much or too little and thus throwing the unit off. The abstinent smoker has a close-order drill team that is all out of sync.

When we combine these sensory changes with the other cognitive effects we've talked about, we begin to get a more complete notion of what "drug addiction" means. Withdrawal from a drug under this view is not simply a one-dimensional state of feeling bad. It is the *sum* of all the negative things that happen to us when we quit taking a drug. If I am an accountant and I have some physical discomfort brought on by stopping smoking, and then I add to that the fact that I'm suddenly having trouble getting through my ledgers, how much worse is that going to make me *feel*? How much more likely to start smoking again?

CHAPTER 6

Absolutely

I<small>F GOING WITHOUT</small> nicotine has these kinds of effects on people, what kinds of performance effects can we expect when smokers have a steady supply of the drug? Does taking it just bring them back to "normal," or is it possible that it gives them an edge on normal? Actually, we can broaden the question: Could nicotine help anyone—smoker or not—pay greater attention to his or her income tax forms, or play chess better, or step on the car brakes faster? In other words, what about the second overarching question we asked earlier: Can nicotine produce *absolute* enhancements in human performance?

Opinions exist all over the place on this question. When we look over the territory, to one side are the strongest proponents of what we might call the *performance, si!* position, British researchers David Warburton and Keith Wesnes of the University of Reading. They have written:

The questions for future research are not whether smoking improves information processing, but why, to what extent, in what ways and in whom.

And:

Smokers learn that smoking produces a clear improvement in mental efficiency which enables them to function better and sustain their performance. This increased mastery of their environment will be a very potent reinforcer of smoking behavior.[1]

On the other side, we have the *performance, no!* position, best exemplified by Stanley Schachter of Columbia University. Schachter has long since stopped doing smoking research, alas, but at one time he was champion of an Occam's razor theory of smoking: that people smoke solely because they're addicted to cigarettes. Thus Schachter on smoking's putative benefits:

Another way of phrasing this same conclusion is that the heavy smoker gets nothing out of smoking. He smokes only to prevent withdrawal. I freely admit that this is a perverse conclusion to reach about a habit that is as costly and universally pervasive as smoking, but the existing data for humans do not encourage any other conclusion.[2]

In between these antipodes are the majority of smoking researchers, whose views we might characterize as *performance, maybe!* My own view lies tentatively in the first camp: that is, the evidence we have indicates that nicotine may well enhance some forms of human performance.

What might we expect of a drug that can stimulate people—arouse them, alert them—in the way we know nicotine does? One thing might be that it could increase a person's ability to concentrate or pay attention. Wesnes and Warburton have carried out some experiments on this topic involving what's commonly known as the Mackworth Clock test. Subjects were isolated in a lab and told to watch the sweep hand of a clock. The trick was that they had to punch a button every time the sweep hand *paused*, which it did for the barest wisp of a moment— three-hundredths of a second. It did this only four times a minute, and at irregular intervals. Paying attention to this for 2 minutes might be daunting enough, but this test went on for 80 minutes.[3] Clearly, these people were being tested on something that was akin to watching grass grow.

As you might expect, people tended to do worse at spotting these pauses as the test went on. Wesnes and Warburton measured three test groups: nonsmokers, deprived smokers (12 hours' abstinence), and smokers who were allowed to smoke at several intervals during the test. The results were that the smokers maintained their performance much better over the 80 minutes than either the nonsmokers or the smoking abstainers. (Sixty minutes into the test, in fact, the smokers were performing as well as they did at its start.)

This same kind of thing has been done with auditory vigilance—listening for particular number sequences—and with other tasks, such as car-driving simulation, and the results have been pretty much the same: nicotine seems to help people maintain their concentration over time. One might wish for *more* evidence supporting this conclusion, but what there is, it seems to me, definitely points in this direction. The operative word here, however, is that it "maintains" concentration, meaning that smoking seems to keep it steady during a task that goes on for awhile. This is a different assertion from saying that it *boosts* concentration and keeps it there. In the studies just mentioned, there was little evidence of this effect.

Evidence for a generalized enhancement of concentration, however, does come from several different sources. Wesnes and Warburton ran another Mackworth Clock experiment, similar to the one above, only this time they used nicotine tablets of varying dosages and gave the drug to nonsmokers as well as smokers. The nicotine improved the smokers' ability to detect pauses, and it lessened the nonsmokers' tendency to hit the button in a false alarm—to signal a pause when none had occurred.[4]

A kind of backdoor support for general concentration enhancement has been provided by Karin Andersson and her colleagues, who in the mid-1970s divided a group of women smokers equally into smokers and abstainers. The two groups then were presented with a series of words that were flashed onto different corners of a screen. The women were told beforehand they were going to be tested on how well they could remember the words—which they were—and no differences between the groups were found. However, when they were then asked, to their surprise, what corner of the screen various words were presented on, the smokers did *worse* than the abstainers. In a second version of the test, though, all the women were told to pay attention to the words *and* their location; with these instructions, the smokers slightly outperformed the abstainers on the location test. One interpretation of this result is that nicotine helps people concentrate on whatever the given task is, while letting incidental information go.[5]

Smokers sometimes speak of tobacco producing a "cocoonlike" effect in them, wrapping them in their private world and shutting out the world around them. In line with this, Ottawa's Verner Knott, who did the work with strobe lights and deprived smokers, has suggested that tobacco may increase attention by acting as a "stimulus filter" and has uncovered several strands of evidence that support this. As measured by EEG, tobacco makes smokers react less strongly to distracting, irrelevant noise when they are carrying out experimental work. Knott found that the EEG response of smokers to a 100-decibel blast of white noise—administered when they were carrying out a reaction-time test—was substantially reduced when they were allowed to smoke.[6] Along the same lines, he has reported that tobacco seems to be able to first enhance attention and then *disengage* it quickly when that's what the task calls for, this whole process occurring in the blink of an eye.[7]

As different as these (and other) findings are, they seem to point to a generalized enhancement of concentration with smoking. This work has a way to go, but I suspect that at the end of the day, this concentration enhancement will be shown to be the case. It goes without saying that concentration capabilities such as these would be very attractive to anyone: to keep attention fixed over a long period of time to some boring, repetitive chore; to focus strongly on what's important and let go of what's not; to filter out the million-and-one distractions that are part of so many working environments. Who wouldn't want these capabilities at his or her fingertips? We saw earlier that tobacco can lay some claim to being a *working* drug; people use it more often during the working day than at any other time. We focused earlier on its emotional effects in this regard: its seeming ability to keep mood on an even keel. Here, it seems to me, is the cognitive side of that mood effect. If borne out, this effect would represent at least one good reason for why people smoke: it helps them take care of business in their daily working lives.

Concentration is only one of a whole constellation of abilities that together are commonly referred to as mental processing. Another ability in this constellation is sometimes known as rapid information processing. It is related to concentration—indeed, almost anything we do has a concentration component to it—but is separate from it nevertheless. Wesnes and Warburton have been the champions of the notion that smoking improves this ability, and for many years now they have carried out a large number of very similar experiments to test that hypothesis.

The basic setup in these tests is that subjects look at a video screen, onto which are flashed a series of numbers. The subjects' task is to hit a button as fast as they can every time they see a series of three consecutive odd or even digits. Since they are seeing 100 numbers per minute, the test becomes an exercise in fast thinking. Because it's computer controlled, this simple experiment can test for several things: the number of correct digit detections, the number of false detections, the speed with which subjects hit the button, and their ability to do all these things *over time.*

When Wesnes and Warburton have tested only smokers, they have obtained some pretty impressive results. When these people are allowed to smoke, their performance is boosted over that during a baseline testing period: they make more correct detections and hit the button faster; furthermore, they maintain their performance over time, which they don't when they are kept from smoking.[8]

We have to be cautious about these results, though, because of our old bugaboo, nicotine withdrawal. That is, you could make a case that Wesnes and Warburton were measuring not an improvement in performance when these people are smoking, but a decline in performance when they are deprived of smoking, however brief this deprivation may be.

One way of controlling for this is to test nonsmokers with nicotine tablets. That's just what Wesnes and Warburton did, and here, while they got some positive results, the findings aren't as strong as when they were measuring smokers only.[9] These findings move in the same direction as the smokers' experiments—the nicotine prevented a decrease in accuracy and speed over time, for example—but they aren't as robust as the other results. What emerges from this work, it seems to me, are some provocative test results—indicating that smoking aids in this kind of mental sprinting—that would benefit from the kind of converging evidence we saw with the concentration studies.

There are several other areas in which claims have been made that nicotine boosts mental efficiency, and a couple of them deserve mention. One is memory and learning. There is a large body of work on this subject—larger perhaps than on any other aspect of nicotine and mental functioning. These studies have involved rats and humans, short-term and long-term memory, difficult and simple material—in short, science has covered a fair amount of territory on this question. If we were to walk through this body of material, though, in the end we'd be left with the feeling that the whole thing is a kind of Mexican standoff: for every study that finds some effect, another finds none or finds a contrary effect. If any one effect consistently is shown, however, it is that, like many drugs, nicotine produces what's called "state-dependent" learning, meaning that if you learn something in a given state—on nicotine, on caffeine, or straight—you remember it better in that state. If so, then this effect would tend to keep people smoking through a never-ending daisy-chain of learning and recalling while on nicotine. But as such, it's not an absolute performance enhancement; if anything, as a motive it belongs in the category of the effects of nicotine withdrawal.

The last area we'll look at here has to do with purely physical perception and movement. At one time or another, most of us have turned on a fan and, as its speed increases, watched the three individual blades in it turn into one ghostly gray mass. In science, there is a kind of analog to this called the critical flicker fusion (CFF) test. Imagine it like this: you sit in a darkened room while watching a light that flickers on and off, slowly at first but then at a greater speed, until at a certain point it ceases to flicker altogether and simply looks like a light that's turned on. The point at which it stops flickering, called the CFF threshold, is a measure of brain arousal and is affected by such things as fatigue.[10] That is, an alert person will see the flicker at a higher rate of speed than will a tired person.

England's Hans Eysenck and K. M. Warwick took a group of 60 smokers and nonsmokers—interestingly, all members of the "genius" society Mensa—and measured their flicker-fusion performance in two states: without nicotine, and with very small doses of it, taken in the form of tablets. The result was that when they were dosed on nicotine they could perceive the flickering at a higher rate.[11]

In another area, researchers in England gave a group of nonsmokers doses of nicotine (in solution, through the nose) and then asked them to tap as fast as they could with their forefinger on a computer keyboard. The result was that when they were on nicotine they could tap about 5 percent faster than when they were not. (How fast can you tap a computer key? About 448 times a minute with nicotine, 427 times without it.) Moreover, this effect was not short-lived: it was still being seen an hour after dosing.[12]

Such physical enhancements as these are small things, unlikely to be of much practical importance to most people, I think, except in the secondary way of making them *feel* a little differently about the way they interact with their environment, with awareness of their different state skimming dolphinlike just above and below consciousness.

One of the reasons I've gone through these things, though, is that I just can't resist speculating that these effects might help explain something that puzzles a large part of the American public: why so many baseball players chew tobacco. It's not just our imagination that a large proportion of major league ballplayers chew: in 1987 G. N. Connolly and his colleagues surveyed 265 of them in seven teams and found that 34 percent used it.[13] The reasons they gave for chewing were the usual: relaxation, habit, dependence. And none of them said it sharpened their reflexes or improved their game. Yet, as we've seen, a lot of the motivation for tobacco use exists at an unconscious level, and we shouldn't be surprised that baseball players, like most people, wouldn't be aware of what tobacco does to them, or for them. (In addition, would we really expect them to *admit* that a drug is doing something for them on the field?) Consistent with what they said, however, Steven Edwards and his colleagues at Oklahoma State University tested a group of college men—some of them athletes—and found that chewing tobacco did not improve their reaction times.[14]

This finding is somewhat at variance with other studies that have measured nicotine's effect on reaction time, but even if we accept the Oklahoma results at face value, it's clear that reaction time is not all there is to athletic performance. Consider this: Jeannette Friedman and Russell Meares in Australia took readings of electrocortical responses to both visual and auditory stimuli (evoked-potential readings) for a group of smokers, and their findings were consistent with the notion that "smoking enhances input into the visual system whereas it 'damps down' or reduces, auditory sensation."[15] They note that other studies with nicotine have shown an increased sensitivity to visual stimuli on the one hand and a screening out of meaningless auditory noise on the other (a la Verner Knott). This sounds to me like a perfect combination for a baseball player who, when batting, must ignore a howling crowd while giving undivided attention to the trajectory of the baseball. Phillip Woodson, who has run evoked-potential experiments with smoking, says that the visual enhancements he observed with it are "attentional" enhancements perfectly consistent with concentrating on a moving ball as it moves from pitcher to batter.[16] The results we've seen on critical flicker fusion and tapping rate are, likewise, consistent with the idea that chewing tobacco might be giving players that little something extra they need to perform well. And in professional athletics, where the differences between a champion and an also-ran are very small, a little something extra can go a long way.

This is all speculative, of course, and it's clear that nicotine has other effects—hand tremor, for example—that are not likely to help anyone hit a fastball. Yet it seems to me that professional baseball ought to look in detail at this question and decide whether it should regard chewing tobacco in the same way as football regards steroid dosing: as an unacceptable use of drugs. Chewing tobacco causes mouth cancer, and its use is rising sharply among American boys. Anyone who has been around young boys knows of the admiration, bordering on reverence, they have for professional baseball players. Given these two things, I think professional baseball would have impetus enough—on public health grounds alone—to limit on-field chewing by players; with the evidence we've seen of tobacco's potential for employment *as a drug* in the game, I should think that baseball would want to look very closely at this whole area.

We can gain some broader perspective on the perceptual and other effects we've looked at by recalling that we earlier saw evidence that nicotine can seemingly move people up or down a sedation-stimulation scale according to how much they take in and the situation in which they take it. Under this view, it's quite possible that the effects we've surveyed—the likelihood of increased concentration; the possibility of enhanced mental processing; the faster physical functioning—can be modified by the smoker *as desired.* That is, the same things wouldn't happen to the same degree every time a person smoked: *different* things would happen, depending on what the smoker wanted, which would make nicotine a kind of all-purpose drug.

Under this view, then, smoking is not just a matter of being shackled to an addiction; it's an aid, a kind of trick if you wish, to help people function. We saw some evidence of this earlier on the emotional side; here we see it on the cognitive side. Such effects as may exist are subtle, and it's clear that Western civilization got along just fine for hundreds of years without them. Moreover, whatever the effects are, they are small in relation to dying from lung cancer or heart disease. But the question here is not what this balance is; the question is what reasons people have for using tobacco, and these things probably should be counted among them.

We have one final area to cover in the way of absolute benefits nicotine provides. This benefit sits apart from all the others we've talked about in that it's not a cognitive addition to human functioning, but it certainly is an addition to the human sense of well-being.

Smoking helps people stay slimmer. It takes off weight and keeps it off. This is not just some sort of folk wisdom, but is a rock-solid conclusion based on a huge body of research.

It's important to note, however, how I phrased the conclusion about nicotine's effect on weight: it takes it off and keeps it off. That is to say, people who start smoking are likely to *lose* weight compared to what their weight would have been had they not smoked, and continuing smokers gain weight less rapidly than do nonsmokers. Moreover, this effect continues as smokers move through life, so that the weight disparity between smokers and nonsmokers increases with age.[17]

This makes nicotine sound like some sort of magic elixir for the omnipresent American problem of too much self—and it does have something of that quality to it—but it is a decidedly *low-grade* elixir. Smokers weigh about 7 pounds less than nonsmokers, and smokers who quit gain an average of about 6 pounds during the year after they stop.

It's worth noting, however, that this is an average: some studies have reported groups of smokers weighing 15 pounds less than comparable groups of nonsmokers, and others have reported groups of smokers gaining an average of 18 pounds in the year after they quit. As with anything in the individual psyche, it may be the extremes of observed change that motivate our behavior. If Molly gained 20 pounds after quitting while Fred gained only 5, it is Molly whom we remember.

We have a good idea that it is the nicotine in tobacco smoke that is causing this weight phenomenon (rather than, say, carbon monoxide) because people who quit smoking gain weight more slowly if they chew nicotine gum. How nicotine achieves this slimming trick has been the subject of a great deal of investigation over time, but only very recently have scientists been able to put together the pieces of this puzzle so that we at least know what major factors are involved.

First, we know that people do eat more when they stop smoking and, notably through the work of Neil Grunberg, we know that nicotine reduces the amount of sweet foods, in particular, that animals or humans consume. It was clear for a long time that food reduction wasn't the total answer to the question, however, because animals that are exposed to cigarette smoke lose weight without reducing their food intake. Furthermore, it seems clear that smokers eat as much or more than nonsmokers while keeping a lower body weight.[18]

This left two prime suspects: that smoking increases physical activity or that it increases metabolic rate. Either way, smokers would burn up more calories than nonsmokers and stay slimmer. It turns out that, if anything, smokers are *less* physically active than nonsmokers, and animal studies bear out the notion that nicotine doesn't have much effect on physical activity. (How can you tell how active animals are? You shine infrared light beams through their cages; the animals block these light beams—much as people block the light beams in elevator doors—and a computer registers each break in the light as a movement. At the end of the day you count up the movements.)

Since physical activity doesn't have much effect, this means that metabolism probably works with changes in food consumption to produce smoking's slimming effect. Up through 1988, however, the evidence was contradictory on metabolism: some studies found that the metabolic rates of smokers would slow when they stopped smoking, but other studies found no such effect.

Then in 1989, Kenneth Perkins and his colleagues produced two studies that went a long way toward answering this question. First, they showed that nicotine produced a small but significant increase of the metabolic rate in people when they are at rest—that is, when they are awake but doing nothing. The researchers wondered, however, how much this could explain about smoking and weight maintenance. As we've seen, we have reason to believe that smokers consume most of their cigarettes when they are at work. Could it be, Perkins's group asked, that the metabolic effect of nicotine during "light activity" might be more important in explaining its slimming effects?

The answer was yes. Perkins took two groups of smokers and gave one of them a standardized dose of nicotine (up the nose), while the other group got a placebo. Then he had both groups alternately rest or pedal lightly on a kind of bicycle apparatus. He found that although nicotine caused more energy to be expended during either rest or pedaling, the absolute excess energy expenditure *caused by the nicotine* was more than twice as great when the smokers were engaged in the light activity. To put this another way, nicotine provides much more of a metabolic bang during activity than during rest.[19]

Perkins noted that his results suggest an explanation for why nicotine seems to affect some smokers' weights so strikingly, while it affects other smokers hardly at all: those who tend to smoke more while active would have their weight most affected by nicotine. On the other hand, those who smoked mostly while relaxing, or on coffee breaks or the like, would stand to be affected very little.

With this research, we now have a pretty good idea of at least the higher level mechanisms involved in nicotine's effect on weight: smokers probably eat a little less, particularly of sweet foods, and they burn up more calories than nonsmokers, particularly if they smoke while active.

But is weight loss or maintenance a reason that people start smoking or keep smoking? The evidence is mixed on this, but the answer seems to be yes. In 1983, Larry Tucker surveyed 400 U.S. high school boys and found that the overweight boys among them were much more likely to say that they intended to smoke than either normal weight or underweight boys.[20] British researcher Anne Charlton surveyed 16,000 schoolchildren in the mid-1980s and found that 42 percent of the heavy smokers agreed that smoking helps control weight; when the same question was asked of students who never smoked, only 17 percent agreed with the statement. The greater the amount of smoking, the greater the agreement with the statement.[21] Robert Klesges and his colleagues questioned a group of longer term smokers in 1987 and found that the best predictor of those who had never attempted to quit smoking was the degree of concern they had with weight control.[22]

One final thing needs to be said about this smoking and weight question: the evidence is almost overwhelming that this issue affects women more than it does men. First of all, there may be an actual difference in the effect of smoking on the weight of women versus its effect on the weight of men. Two of three studies we have report that the smoker/nonsmoker weight differences are greater in women than in men, and we have reason to believe that women who quit smoking increase their food consumption more than do men who quit. Second, whether or not this disparity is real, women and girls are certainly more *concerned* about the question of smoking and weight than are men. The 1988 Surgeon General's report noted that females are particularly worried about weight gains after they quit smoking; they are more likely to endorse smoking as a weight-loss strategy; and they are more likely to report relapse to smoking because of weight-related motives.

The reasons for this disparity probably should lie beyond the scope of this book, but we haven't let this kind of thing stop us before, so let's touch on one of them. Robert Klesges conducted a study with 223 subjects and found that overweight females were more accurate than overweight males in reporting the degree of their obesity. Conversely, normal and underweight females reported that they weighed more than they actually did, while normal and underweight males were very accurate about where they stood on the ideal weight scale.[23] The reasons for *this* are fascinating to speculate on, but really do lie outside the scope of this book.

For our purposes, suffice it to say that the arena of smoking seems to provide additional evidence for the assertion that women's concern, perhaps obsession, with weight in this country should be a feminist issue. Lung cancer has now surpassed breast cancer as the most common form of cancer in American women. Adolescent girls now smoke at rates *greater* than the rates for adolescent boys. We can infer from the evidence we have seen that the fear of weight is probably responsible to some extent for these depressing events. To the degree that women keep smoking because of their fears about weight, they are dying because of their fears about weight. (Whatever health benefits a woman may derive from losing 7 pounds are overwhelmed by the disastrous physical effects of smoking.) Since nearly one-quarter of all adult American women smoke, this is not a trivial matter: some 46,000 American women were diagnosed with lung cancer in 1985[24] and we can expect that 85 percent of those women are dead today.

As usual, the tobacco industry has weighed in on an important tobacco issue in the wrong way. At one time, the industry was blatant in advertising appeals that linked smoking with a thinner female figure. ("Reach for a Lucky instead of a sweet" is one of the memorable advertising slogans of the 1920s.) Now it simply plasters pictures of beautiful, ultrathin women selling ultrathin cigarettes on print ads and billboards across the country. The obvious, unstated message is that smoking equals thinness. And, as we have seen, to some degree it does. American advertising is one large dream machine, of course, and Big Tobacco is no more to blame for playing on this than are other advertisers. The problem is that the stakes are so high with this product. The risk is not of buying a product that you don't need, but of buying a product that can addict and kill you. To echo the words of another writer, it seems clear that smoking is a feminist issue.

· · ·

When we step back and look at the effects of nicotine on day-to-day human functioning—both the weight loss and the constellation of cognitive effects we've reviewed—it's worth noting that the debate on nicotine has been framed almost entirely in terms of what *enhancements* it may provide. Debilitations are found here and there with nicotine, but in the main the question has been: Does nicotine do something positive, or does it do nothing at all? This is pretty remarkable when you consider the *maladaptive* effects of most recreational drugs. Information processing and alcohol? Concentration and heroin? Memory and marijuana? By now, though, readers may have come to expect this, since a general theme that has emerged in our discussion is that nicotine is a drug, but a very strange one. We turn now, however, to the first part of that formulation. Our theme here could be: A drug is a drug is a drug.

CHAPTER 7

Controlling the Ship's Captain

To LOTS OF people who have given up smoking—or to those who have merely been around these people—it may seem absurd that there was ever a debate about whether or not smoking is addictive. After all, three-quarters of all smokers say they would like to stop. They presumably are saying this *despite* whatever benefits they derive from it. What's keeping them from following through? As a clue, people who have tried to quit have given us plenty of descriptions like this:

> I'm telling you I wanted a cigarette so bad I cried. I did. And not just once but several times. I was so nervous I could hardly carry on at work, and I couldn't hide it. After awhile I would just shake. People said they couldn't see it, but I could feel it.[1]

This is obviously a bit different from what happens when a person is deprived of, say, his favorite breakfast cereal, and therefore it seems a little ridiculous on the face of it to say that there is nothing more going on here than a keen appreciation of tobacco.

On the other hand, all things are relative. Here is a paraphrase taken from researcher Jerome Jaffe's description of heroin withdrawal:

> Symptoms include insomnia, marked anorexia, violent yawning, severe sneezing, weakness and depression, nausea and vomiting, intestinal spasm and diarrhea. Heart rate and blood pressure are elevated; there is a marked chilliness, alternating with flushing and excessive sweating. The addict experiences waves of gooseflesh, his skin resembling that of a plucked turkey, which is the basis of the expression "cold turkey." Abdominal cramps and pains in the bones and muscles of the back and extremities are characteristic, as are muscle spasms and kicking movements that may be the basis for the expression "kicking the habit." Other signs include ejaculations in men and orgasm in women. The failure to take foods and fluids, combined with vomiting, sweating, and diarrhea, results in marked weight loss and dehydration. Occasionally, there is cardiovascular collapse.[2]

So we're definitely talking about different levels of voodoo when we speak of withdrawal from these two drugs; because of this, the question might naturally arise as to whether nicotine withdrawal actually represents a true drug withdrawal at all.

Moreover, withdrawal symptoms are only one measure of addiction or, to be more precise, physical dependence. There is a whole range of standardized tests that science uses to establish whether a drug is liable to cause physical dependence and, up through the 1970s, it wasn't clear whether nicotine passed or flunked some of these tests.

Even so, it may not be apparent why science had to go to a great deal of trouble to prove what the person on the street thought to be the case anyway, but there are good reasons for this. First, even as an abstract question, this issue could not be settled except by science, for it is only in the laboratory, in the realm of precise dosages and statistical significance, that opinion and folklore could be separated from fact. Common sense may tell us that smoking is addictive, but common sense also told generations of Europeans that babies weighed an average of about 12 pounds at birth.

Second, this is not simply an academic question. In terms of public policy—federal and state laws, regulatory agency actions, and the like—it matters whether or not smoking is addictive. To take but one example, the late 1980s debate over whether R. J. Reynolds's ill-fated "smokeless cigarette," Premier, should be regulated by the FDA had to do with whether the product was simply a delivery system for an *addictive* drug.

Beyond this, the question of nicotine's addictive powers does not exist in a vacuum. There is a well-heeled group of spokesmen who would like nothing better than for the public to believe that nicotine is *not* addictive. The tobacco industry fought tooth and nail—successfully, it turned out—to keep the current Surgeon General's warnings from containing the word "addictive." The industry is thought to fear the addiction label partly because of what it might do to its legal position in product liability suits. Beyond this, however, Big Tobacco wants to be seen as just another American business, giving the public what it wants in the way of a consumer product. But the addiction label puts it squarely in another camp: the lizard-eyed world of drug pandering. The fact of tobacco use as an addiction makes plain that while tobacco's gleaming corporate offices may reach to the stars, they are built on a foundation that is beneath contempt: the supplying of a product to a clientele who must continue to use it or suffer mentally and physically.

As it turns out, the Surgeon General's warning battle is the only fight tobacco companies have won in this realm in recent years. The World Health Organization, the American Psychiatric Association, the American Public Health Association, the National Institute on Drug Abuse, and finally the Surgeon General have all independently concluded that smoking is addictive. (The Surgeon General can issue a finding about this on his own hook; to change the Surgeon General's warning on cigarette packs, though, requires an act of Congress, which acts, of course, not on the basis of truth, but of political muscle.) So this issue is settled; there are fine points to be debated here and there, but there is no "controversy" over whether smoking is addictive.

How do we know about the addictive power of nicotine? Well, first of all, it's now clear that smoking—this seemingly random, directionless act—is extremely regular and controlling, which are the very hallmarks of addictive drug use. This is so much the case that we could imagine addiction as a kind of drill sergeant, giving orders on smoking to a bunch of new nicotine enlistees:

> Recruits, you'll find that smoking will make you nauseous at first, but you will keep with it, and smoke a little more with each passing month until you level out your consumption, usually at about 20 cigarettes a day, and hold this pattern for years, maybe a lifetime. That's your long-term picture. In the short run, the cigarettes you smoke will be evenly spaced out over time; likewise for the drags you take within each cigarette. The main thing is you will take in the same amount of nicotine each day. Do not attempt to vary this amount because it will not work. If you cut down on the number of cigarettes you smoke, you'll find that you just increase the number of drags on the cigarettes you do smoke. If you try to take fewer drags on the cigarettes you smoke, you'll just end up smoking more cigarettes.[3]

So things are regular with smoking. Smokers don't capriciously decide to have a cigarette. Within a certain loose framework, they're obliged to have one. Here we reach the nic-o-stat concept with which our whole discussion started, and we can see that there's some truth to it.

This fact is exemplified through a very common practice: the smoking of "low-tar, low-nicotine" cigarettes. These cigarettes are so named from the Federal Trade Commission rating process begun in 1967. The notion is, of course, that people who can't quit smoking can at least cut down on the amount of tar and nicotine they take in by smoking "light" cigarettes, and the FTC method of rating can give these smokers a benchmark to decide which cigarettes fall into this category.

Even today, I think, most people believe that the tobacco in these cigarettes *contains* less tar and nicotine, in the same way that skim milk contains less fat. It doesn't (which the cigarette companies undoubtedly knew all along). Instead, these cigarettes get low FTC-method ratings because of features like their ventilation holes—which dilute the tobacco smoke with plain air—and the speed with which their tobacco burns. These features allow these cigarettes to *deliver* less tar and nicotine to FTC-calibrated smoking machines—but not necessarily to people. Why? Because people do what FTC machines cannot: block the ventilation holes, smoke the cigarettes farther down, take more intense drags. People do this because of what we talked about above: they need a certain amount of nicotine to keep the Nag at bay and will get it one way or another even from low-nicotine cigarettes. It is not till you get to *ultra-low* cigarettes that these techniques will not work. And what's the result in this case? Poor sales for ultra-lows because they don't deliver the goods, no matter how they are manipulated.*

The evidence from this whole subindustry, then, is in perfect keeping with the notion that smokers require a certain level of nicotine day in and day out. This realm of evidence is familiar to us because it deals with products we see in our everyday lives. A good deal of the evidence on the addictive nature of smoking, however, comes from the rarified environment of the laboratory.

Let's say it's 1980, and the white-coat fellows from the medical establishment—who are worried about this little business of 360,000 Americans dying each year from smoking—say that they think tobacco is addictive. Meanwhile, the pinstripe boys from the tobacco industry say: nonsense, it's relaxing, refreshing, and so on. Well, both these parties have axes to grind on this issue, so where are we going to get an objective view of this—one not tainted by societal prejudices? How

---

*Three sets of researchers in particular were responsible for blowing the whistle on this whole low-tar sham: Lynn Kozlowski and his colleagues at the Addiction Research Foundation in Toronto, Neal Benowitz and Peyton Jacob III and their colleagues at the University of California, San Francisco, and Britain's M. A. H. Russell. Kozlowski brought attention to "hole-blocking," and he has pointed out how effective it and other techniques can be in delivering nicotine and tar. To take an admittedly extreme case, doing these things has turned a John Players King Size Ultra Mild—nominally rated at 0.8 milligram tar—into a fag delivering 28.5 milligrams of tar.[4] This is nearly as much of this carcinogenic sludge as you would have gotten smoking a straight Camel about 1955.

None of this is to say, however, that smokers might just as well smoke straight Camels. Epidemiological evidence shows clear reductions in lung cancer for smokers who, years ago, began smoking filtered, lower yield cigarettes. Chronic lung diseases like emphysema *may* be reduced by smoking lower yield cigarettes. Heart disease is another matter, however. There is no evidence of a difference in heart attack risk for smokers of lower yield cigarettes.[5] (One of the likely culprits in heart disease is carbon monoxide, which low-yield cigarettes cut down on only somewhat.) Overall, however, with just plain low-tar, low-nicotine cigarettes, people *may* reduce their intake of poisons, though this is kind of a crapshoot, since a fair amount of their consumption process goes on at an unconscious level. Given the stakes, though, smokers are clearly better off betting on low-tar and nicotine cigarettes if they can't quit altogether.

about from monkeys, rats, and dogs? Not only do they not have opinions about the question, but they presumably have never been influenced by a Marlboro ad or a Virginia Slims billboard.

How do we get them to tell us anything? Well, first of all, we see if they'll *work* for the supposedly addictive drug in tobacco, nicotine. Not work too hard; just press a lever to get it. If they press the lever a lot—repeatedly, frequently—then we have a pretty good idea that it's doing something for them. In scientific terms, the nicotine is *reinforcing* their behavior. It is motivating them to do something—lever pressing— that they wouldn't do otherwise. (I can't help but see in these tests a crystalline reduction of the human situation. What will people do to get their drugs? Walk two blocks out of their way, already late for an appointment, to get a pack of cigarettes?)

The king of reinforcing drugs for this test is cocaine. Given un- limited access to it (through IV injections), rats will press the cocaine levers, forsaking food or sex or anything else, until they die. People are quite fond of it too in this setting. (On the other hand, animals and people are often indifferent to caffeine in these tests and are actually averse to LSD—so much so that another name for a *dysphoria* scale in drug testing is the LSD scale; if people tell you this drug is addictive, tell them it's highly unlikely.)

From the earliest nicotine tests, in 1967, it was clear that animals would press levers for it, but their *rates* of pressing were so low that it called into question the whole notion of nicotine being reinforcing. Then in 1981, Steven Goldberg of the National Institute on Drug Abuse (NIDA) discovered that he simply had to fine-tune the nicotine delivery somewhat to see that it worked quite well as a reinforcer.[6] Not as well as cocaine, but clearly it lay in the realm of reinforcing drugs. When Goldberg made nicotine available on an intermittent basis, and sometimes flashed on a small light as it was delivered, he found that squirrel monkeys would hit the lever as many as 250 times to get a single injection.

The Goldberg experiment turned out to lie right at the beginning of a comprehensive set of studies on the addictive potential of nicotine carried out through the 1980s under the leadership of Goldberg and Jack Henningfield at NIDA's Addiction Research Center (ARC) in Baltimore.* (See footnote on next page.)

One of the things these scientists did was to extend Goldberg's animal findings to human beings. They took some human volunteers—cigarette smokers—put catheters in their arms, and had them sit in a chair for three hours at a time with a radio playing and magazines to read. To the side was a machine with a couple of levers on it; one of the levers didn't do anything, but the other was set up to deliver either nicotine or a saline solution. When nicotine was delivered, these people would press the bar for it at nice, regular intervals. At a certain dose of nicotine per injection, they'd press at about the same rate in each three-hour session, but if the dose were increased—if they got more per shot—they'd reach less frequently for the lever. That they weren't simply interested in lever pressing or the experience of fluid injection is shown by what happened when (unbeknownst to them) saline was used: the lever pressing was disordered and unpredictable and decreased as the sessions went on.[7] If you don't get what you want, you cease to work for it.

Part of what the ARC workers did could be subsumed under a research heading that might be called "Ask the experts." In the same way that a wine connoisseur might be blindfolded and asked about the bouquet of a 1979 Pinot Noir, so the ARC workers went out and got drug experts—guys who had been junkies or speed freaks, or junkies *and* speed freaks and whatever else—to find out if (*a*) nicotine did anything for them and (*b*) what other drugs it felt like. These men received doses of a whole range of drugs, from the familiar (morphine) to the exotic (zomepirac), and their responses were calibrated on a "liking" scale developed by the ARC. With neither the researchers nor the subjects aware of what drug was being given at any particular time, the drug veterans reacted to nicotine in the same way as they did to morphine or amphetamine: they liked it a lot, and the more they got of it the better they liked it. And what drug did they most often think it was? Cocaine.[8]

Drugs of abuse generally cause withdrawal, which in the most general terms we can define as a negative state brought on by the lack of a drug. (As

* That this work was able to get going at all was due in large part to the efforts of Joseph Califano, the first Secretary of the Department of Health, Education, and Welfare under Jimmy Carter. Califano was forthright about the health effects of tobacco; in consequence he was an anathema to the tobacco industry and was subsequently fired. His stand on tobacco, however, made it acceptable for money to be funneled to NIDA to study nicotine as a drug.

the literary formulation has it: what once were vices now are necessities.) We've seen evidence already that smokers perform worse at certain tasks when they are deprived of nicotine. But is there a general, predictable nicotine withdrawal syndrome? Given tobacco's ubiquity and its devastating health effects, it's surprising, perhaps, that we didn't have a definitive answer to this question until fairly recently. Heroin withdrawal has been well documented since the 1940s, and alcohol withdrawal since the 1950s. But nearly 20 years went by between the first Surgeon General's report on smoking in 1964 and a comprehensive series of studies on smoking withdrawal conducted by Dorothy Hatsukami and John Hughes and their colleagues at the University of Minnesota.

Hatsukami and Hughes got serious about this by taking a group of smokers, housing them on a clinical research ward, and then measuring them around the clock for three days before they quit and for four days after they did.[9] These people were scrutinized from top to bottom: their vital signs were taken; their sleep interruptions were noted; even their levels of physical activity were measured via monitors placed around their waists. The researchers took account of both objective measurements (hand tremor, heart rate) and subjective reports (how depressed or nervous people said they were).

Hatsukami and Hughes then followed this up by doing much the same thing with smokers trying to quit out in the real world—that is to say, quitting just as most people do, only with the addition of the testing and analysis.[10]

From this, the researchers came up with a short list of the withdrawal symptoms that were reliably seen in both settings: increased number of awakenings during sleep, increased confusion, increased craving for tobacco, increased eating, and decreased heart rate.[11] When we look only at the inpatient study, however, we see all this plus increased body weight and increased depression and dejection in subjective mood states. When we look only at the outpatient study, we also get such things as increased anger and hostility and increased tension and anxiety. Overall, there were a greater number of changes in the outpatient condition, which is not surprising, for reasons we'll go into later.

What do these dry, clinical terms actually mean? Well, Hatsukami and Hughes put some perspective on this by observing that in their outpatient study, the psychological tests the abstainers took put them in the 40th to 50th percentile of psychiatric outpatients. "Thus, during abstinence," they say, "the subjects were as distressed as the average psychiatric outpatient."[12]

This sounds about right. Confusion, craving, depression, hostility. Not physical and psychological collapse, as with heroin, but not normal either by a long shot. What proportion of quitters feel these effects? It's hard to say; most of the people in the outpatient study reported experiencing five or more symptoms, but a review of many such studies indicates that perhaps one-quarter of all smokers who quit report no withdrawal whatsoever.[13] My guess is that a standard distribution goes on, with a minority of quitters having no trouble, the majority in the middle having a fair amount of difficulty, and a minority over at the other end in a state of misery.

How long does this go on? It's generally agreed that withdrawal comes on within a matter of hours and peaks within two or three days. Within this time, confusion and anxiety are lessened, and sleep interruptions are fewer.

Withdrawal is regarded by most people, I think, as the black beast at the heart of drug addiction, be it to heroin, cocaine, or cigarettes. That is to say, it is regarded as the single most important reason people cannot quit taking drugs. Yet is it withdrawal—short-term punishment for not taking a drug—that really is central to addiction?

The symptoms of withdrawal may decline after a few days, but it is a false sunrise that greets the reformed smoker a week or so after quitting. Thereupon begins the more subtle—and because of this more insidious—"protracted abstinence" syndrome. The scientific literature contains reports of ex-smokers having intermittent, intense urges to smoke up to nine years after quitting; my guess is that these desires may exist for a lifetime in some people.

Studies of long-term quitting rates confirm that protracted abstinence is much more of a minefield for ex-smokers than is immediate withdrawal. Stop-smoking clinics have, over the years, been successful in getting 60 to 80 percent of their enrollees to quit during the few days to weeks that they are in session.[14] Then begins the plunge: during the first three months after the program, 65 percent of those who quit will have returned to smoking. After a year, 75 percent of those who quit are smoking again. It's worth noting that heroin addicts and alcoholics relapse at almost exactly this same rate.[15]*

The *months* following quitting, then, are the long march for a great number of ex-smokers, and in this syndrome we can see, I think, the true depressive dilemma that comes with this brand of drug addiction. Protracted abstinence is the intermittent tug on the sleeve, the feeling in the chest, the whisper in the ear saying how good it would be to have just one cigarette. But one cigarette for a lot of ex-smokers means they're gone; it means they're back to life on the other plane. Back to the endless cycle of need and satiation, in which they get to carry on unhindered for only 40 minutes at a time, at which point they have to return to mother nicotine to receive permission to remain themselves. Without this homage, the smoker begins to turn into something slightly different: a person desirous of his controller, edgy, hostile, depressed, confused. Behold man.

---

*These results are somewhat suspect because they represent a sample of people who, in most cases, made a single attempt to quit one drug or another after coming to clinics for treatment. We know that in the case of smoking the vast majority of people who quit do so on their own—almost always after moving between smoking and not smoking for awhile. Stanley Schachter found that among two groups he sampled, about 64 percent were able to give up smoking, sometimes after several attempts at quitting. On the other hand, M. A. H. Russell has reported that only 35 percent of regular smokers succeed in giving up permanently before the age of 60, even though the vast majority would like to stop.[16]

CHAPTER 8

Inside the Black Box

WE HAVE NOW seen a good deal of evidence indicating that smoking cigarettes is not so much different from other forms of drug use. It is regular, it is controlling, it has its own withdrawal syndrome, and so forth. From this evidence, we have a good idea of what it means to be a nicotine user and then to try to quit being one. Yet how much does this tell us, really? To say *that* withdrawal happens is not to say *why* it happens. In the evidence we've reviewed so far, human beings have been like the mysterious black box: you put certain substances like nicotine in one side, and you get certain effects, like addiction and withdrawal, out the other. But what is happening inside the box to make this take place?

Inside the box. There are a million external influences on smoking, or the taking of any addictive drug. But let's set these things aside for the moment and concentrate on the inside of the box; let's look, in other words, at what we know about the biological basis of addiction, concentrating first on withdrawal.

The common thread that runs through most theories of withdrawal is that the body seeks *stasis*—it seeks to remain as it is—and accordingly will modify itself to remain the same when chronically pushed in a new direction by a drug. It's rather like a house that is pushed in the direction of cold by the winds of January; the thermostat in the house works against this external influence to keep the home's internal environment the same. The body has, in a sense, a multitude of small thermostats that push in the opposite direction from external drug influences.

The pharmacological concept that describes this phenomenon is *tolerance*, normally a good thing in human affairs, but with a slightly different meaning in biology. Pharmacological tolerance means having to take progressively more of a given drug to keep getting the same effect from it. The prime example of this is in heroin usage: people who are just starting out with it require only a little to get very high; later on they will require a lot to feel the same way; still later they will require even more just to stave off withdrawal. (There probably are perfectly good evolutionary reasons for why the body reacts this way to drugs, but I prefer a metaphysical explanation: the universe is inherently puritanical; it doesn't mind us getting high, but it doesn't want us to stay that way.)

Nicotine has its own forms of tolerance, but, as we might expect, its tolerance is more subtle than that of the opiates. Its most famous tolerance effect is that kids don't *keep* getting nauseous from smoking once they take it up; there are other effects as well, however. Smokers are unaware of it, but they metabolize nicotine and other drugs faster than do nonsmokers. (Caffeine is one of these; Valium is another: smokers may require up to half again as much Valium as nonsmokers to get the same level of tranquilization.)[1]

Then, too, there is a kind of short-term tolerance, called *tachyphylaxis*, that comes with each day's smoking. Remember how we observed that the first few cigarettes of the day quicken the pulse in smokers, while subsequent cigarettes fail to raise it any further. Acute tolerance is at work here, and its effects on several systems probably explain why so many smokers agree that the first cigarette of the day is the best one.

In general terms, the effect of tolerance is that the body initiates what might be called compensatory activities in response to the chronic presence of its foreign guest, the drug. If the drug pushes in one direction—toward, say, sedation with the opiates—the compensatory activity pushes in the other. To illustrate this with opiates, recall what we looked at earlier about the nervous system's receptors—the chemical sites across the synaptic gaps that act as the doors of transmission. Well, it turns out that the body has its own specialized receptors for opiates. As you might guess, evolution didn't develop these receptors in human beings so that we could process the morphine manufactured from poppy plants. (This would be rather like evolution having developed a special digestive enzyme for pizza.) These receptors were constructed, rather, to deal with the body's *internal* morphines—its *endorphins,* which are neurotransmitters that play a part in the regulation of a wide array of bodily functions. It just so happens that heroin is chemically similar enough to endorphins that it is granted entree when it comes knocking at the door of the opiate receptors.

When a person floods his body with external opiates, the body reacts by reducing the number of these receptor sites. Thus begins a vicious circle in which more heroin leads to fewer receptors, which means even *more* heroin to get the same effect, and the downward spiral continues to its conclusion. Furthermore, while this is going on, the addict's excitatory mechanisms are becoming hyperproductive, trying to overcome the effects of this sedating alien in the body. It also may be the case that the body cuts its endorphin production when it is infused with external opiates.

Suppose, though, that in the middle of this, our addict's supply of heroin is cut off suddenly and completely. *Now* he gets it. His newly powerful excitatory mechanisms run riot, with no sedating drug to oppose them and a reduced number of opiate receptors available for the body's natural sedatives, the endorphins (which may now be in reduced supply anyway). What's the result? Insomnia, a pounding heart, sweating, anxiety—withdrawal effects that move precisely in the opposite direction from the sedated state our user kept trying to put himself in.

There actually is a more pointed example of this syndrome: junkies are constipated; in withdrawal they have diarrhea.

A similar process is at work with nicotine. Chronic infusions of it lead to an increase in the number of nicotinic receptors, but probably to a decrease in the total number of receptors that actually are at work. Furthermore, nicotine withdrawal fits in with our notion of compensatory processes. What kind of withdrawal would we expect from a drug like nicotine that has both depressant and stimulant qualities? Think of what Hatsukami and Hughes observed: on the one hand, increased anxiety and sleeplessness, which would be consistent with withdrawing from a sedative; on the other, decreased heart rate and increased confusion, which we might expect in a person withdrawing from a stimulant. The depressed brain-wave states that Verner Knott has observed would likewise be expected from someone withdrawing from an up-drug.

Withdrawal is clearly only part of the story in drug use, however. It is, if you like, the stick in a carrot-and-stick operation. Furthermore, withdrawal comes later. People don't start out addicted to drugs; they take drugs initially because these substances do something *for* them. We've already had a pretty good look at what nicotine does for human beings in behavioral terms. It seems to allow them to move up or down the sedation-stimulation scale, for example; it may act as a tranquilizer; it may increase the smoker's ability to concentrate: and so forth. We've also had a look at some of the biology beneath these effects: nicotine's ability to serve in the place of the natural neurotransmitter acetylcholine.

What we have not talked about in this regard, however, is what might be called the biology of pure reward. As I write this, one of the hotter topics in psychopharmacology is the notion that a single neurotransmitter and a single "reward pathway" are employed by our most serious drugs of abuse. Dozens of scientists are working on this topic, but the case for such a system—proceeding from the long-standing notion of "pleasure centers" in the brain—has been put forward most forcefully by a Canadian researcher named Roy Wise.

The neurotransmitter in this system, appropriately enough, is dopamine. This substance is vitally important to human beings in domains completely separate from drugs, for it is a lack of dopamine, in an area of the brain called the *corpus striatum,* that causes the rigidity and shaking of Parkinson's disease. The dopamine that comes to the corpus striatum is generated in an area deep in our "primitive" midbrain called the *substantia nigra* (or "black substance," so named because it is dark brown or black).[2] There are two other primary dopamine-producing areas nearby, however: the hypothalamus, and something called the *ventral tegmental* area. It is the last of these that concerns us here.

The ventral tegmental area, in our midbrain, sends forward nerve projections, up and out toward the forehead, in a kind of coaxial cable called the *medial forebrain bundle.* There may be 50 different nerve pathways in this bundle, which has been compared to a frayed rope. Among these fibers are the pathways for dopamine; for our purposes, the most important of these fibers—some of the frays in the rope—go to an area called the *nucleus accumbens.* To repeat, then: dopamine is created in the ventral tegmental area and goes out through the medial forebrain bundle to the nucleus accumbens. Here is the case for how this system is involved in drug addiction, according to Roy Wise.[3]

First, both cocaine and amphetamine increase the levels of dopamine at the synaptic gaps in the nucleus accumbens, though they do this in slightly different ways. Second, without this effect, cocaine and amphetamine cease to be desirable. How do we know? If you give an animal a chemical that will block dopamine receptors—a chemical that will occupy the dopamine doorways—cocaine and amphetamine cease to be attractive to it. (Animals simply stop pressing levers to get it.) You get the same effect when you leave the dopamine receptors un-blocked, but destroy the fibers that carry dopamine to the nucleus accumbens.

Opiates can be brought into this picture as well. Heroin, morphine, and the like also have the effect of raising dopamine levels at the accumbens synapses by causing the dopamine cells to fire more often. Further, it's clear that the ventral tegmental area (the dopamine generator) and the accumbens are important in opiate use: block opiate receptors in the ventral tegmental area and you reduce the attractiveness of IV heroin.

What about nicotine? Work done by several teams of researchers has shown that nicotine causes the release of dopamine into this same system.[4] What has not yet been done with nicotine is the other side of the coin: establishing that this system needs to be functioning for nicotine to be rewarding. It also appears that alcohol increases the dopamine concentration in the ventral tegmental area.

Now, what's crucial to note about Wise's argument is that this medial forebrain system is concerned only with positive reinforcement; that is, it has to do only with the things these various drugs do *for* people. Relief from the withdrawal that we looked at before is *negative* reinforcement—it has to do with people taking drugs to keep things they *don't* like from happening to them (such as sleeplessness, tension, diarrhea). In Wise's view, this positive dopamine system is separate from the several areas of the brain that seem to be involved in negative reinforcement.

Furthermore, just as we noted that opiate receptors didn't evolve in humans to allow us to process manufactured morphine, so this dopamine reward system didn't evolve to allow people to get a bang out of drugs in general. In Wise's view, it is a reinforcement system for natural behaviors that have survival value. Block dopamine release and animals will work less for food and water, even when hungry or thirsty. Inject opiates into the ventral tegmental area or the nucleus accumbens, on the other hand, and you stimulate feeding. Under this view, then, this system is in place to tell us when we are doing the right things; it is reward made corporeal.

What nature has constructed, however, man bends to his own purposes. Centuries ago, the Incas discovered that they could make themselves feel better by chewing coca leaves, achieving this satisfaction, this thesis holds, by increasing the concentration of dopamine in the middle of their brains. Then, 130 years ago, man's newly refined skills in organic chemistry allowed him to distill the psychoactive essence of the coca leaf in the form of pure cocaine. About six years ago, some American entrepreneurs discovered a way to make a cheap, smokable form of cocaine, and the crack plague was upon us.

Progress marches on. Within our biological paradigm here, each of these discoveries meant finding ways to release ever greater, ever more unnatural amounts of dopamine in the nucleus accumbens and thus wrest from a drug every scintilla of reward our bodies could muster. Wise has pointed out that, given this view, it's understandable why drug habits are so hard to break:

If drugs of abuse activate positive reinforcement mechanisms directly and centrally, they may do so with much greater intensity than can ever be summoned by environmental stimuli like food, water, or the reinforcing beauty of nature, art, or music. Whereas the signals from natural reinforcers depend on sensory transducers and the propagation of nerve impulses across axons and synaptic junctions, drugs can activate reinforcement mechanisms centrally, saturating receptor mechanisms that may never be saturated as a consequence of natural reinforcement.[5]

This brings us to two final powerful ideas that stem from Wise's hypothesis. One is that, within this theory, we can provide a tentative answer to the question we asked above: Why is the difficulty with drugs not so much getting off them, but staying off? It may be, Wise says, that because these substances are so powerfully reinforcing, we're going to have a powerful hunger to experience their effects again and again purely from our memory of them:

Craving for cocaine or heroin may, like craving for nicotine in a smoker who has been nicotine free for many years, simply be triggered by memories of past experience. Like a cat that has tasted fish, a human that has tasted cocaine may be unwilling to give up the hope of repeating the experience.[6]

Finally, should the medial forebrain hypothesis be even partly correct, it would go a long way toward explaining one of the best documented and least understood aspects of drug use: the multiple drug abuser. Ninety percent of all alcoholics smoke, and the percentage of opiate addicts who are smokers may be even higher. An appalling number of junkies have problems with alcohol. In general, those who abuse one drug are at very high risk of abusing several. If the dopamine hypothesis is correct, this would be understandable because all of these drugs are employing the same neural circuitry and producing something of the same effect. To put it in terms a cautious scientist never would, they are all yielding *the same high* to a certain degree.

In this regard, it's worth looking at another lever-pressing result pointed out by Wise. Animals that have been trained to press a lever for cocaine can have this behavior "extinguished" by loading up the IV with saline. (After awhile they get the picture and just lose interest in what's coming through the tube.) The lever pressing can be reinstated, however, by giving these animals doses of *morphine* into the ventral tegmental area. They'll start pressing the lever again, just as if they had received a shot of the cocaine they had been addicted to. The implication is that taking any one of the drugs in this class may put someone at risk of relapsing to *another* drug that he formerly abused. Under this view, the ex-alcoholic may make his road even tougher by continuing to smoke cigarettes.

What credence should we give to the dopamine hypothesis? There seems to be a growing consensus among drug researchers that dopamine and the medial forebrain bundle are indeed involved in all the drug addictions we've talked about. Exactly what is meant by the weasel-word "involved," however, is unclear at this point. Given the terrifying complexity of the brain and the drugs in question, many researchers are extremely skeptical of the notion that any one system will turn out to be responsible, even in some substantial part, for our worst drug addictions. Lots of objections can be raised to this hypothesis; any theory so overarching and audacious is bound to attract critics, and Wise certainly has his.

I have gone into such detail on this theory not because I believe it to be true, though it may be, but because it is the most compelling attempt I have seen to turn a vast body of disparate research results into a coherent theory of the biology of reward in drug abuse. This is in itself an achievement that is rather hopeful: a certain critical mass of raw information has to exist before such theories can be produced. Once created, they then serve as organizing principles that can be tested through yet more research. Wise's theory is, then, an example of what I hope we can look forward to more of in the future: testable notions of what drug addiction means at a biological level. Work on this subject is important not just as an academic matter. As we will see later, it's possible that it could have great bearing on the approach that we, as a society, take in dealing with the question of drug abuse.

CHAPTER 9

Gimme That Stuff

For some time now, we've been following a line of reasoning that holds that the use of nicotine is, in some ways, not much different from the use of any other addictive drug. In May 1988, U.S. Surgeon General C. Everett Koop gave the American people this message when he released the nation's 20th report on the health consequences of smoking. Because such announcements have to avoid the tedium of detail, however, the form in which most Americans received this news must have left them a little skeptical of the findings ("Koop to Nation: Cigarettes as Addictive as Heroin"). After all, the smokers around them were nothing like the drug addicts they had seen pictured on TV. How could this be true? With the cocaine wars raging at the time, even the astute Robert MacNeil, interviewing Koop about the report, was incredulous as he listened to the Surgeon General lay out the case that nicotine controls smokers in much the same way that heroin controls junkies.

We've now gone over reasons from the behavioral to the biological indicating that this is the case. One additional view of this question might help round out the picture, however. In terms of the extremes to which the need for drugs will push people, the biggest difference between nicotine and other addictive drugs is that nicotine is legal while the others are not.* Thus, thanks to the efficiencies of legal man-ufacture, a cigarette costs less than 10 cents, while a "rock" of cocaine may cost $10, even though both objects keep their users satisfied for about the same amount of time. Therefore, if you are paying $200 a day for cocaine and are poor to begin with, you live in squalor and rob people or kill them or do whatever is necessary to get that drug into your system. A nicotine habit, on the other hand, can be taken care of with a minimum-wage job.

Despite this, however, there have been times in history when nicotine's delivery vehicle, tobacco, has been unavailable—or available only at the most extreme monetary or human costs. In these rare instances, we get to see what would happen if nicotine were contraband like heroin, and hence a scarce and precious commodity. We begin with Robert Hughes's account of life among the prisoners of the penal colony that was Australia early in the 19th century. Life admittedly was worth far less there than in most times and places. Still, as Hughes reports:

> A group of prisoners were being led in single file through the forest when, without provocation or warning, one of them crushed the skull of the prisoner in front of him with his ax. Later he explained that there was no tobacco to be had in the settlement; that he had been a smoker all his life and would rather die than go without it; so, in the torment of nicotine withdrawal, he had killed the man in order to be hanged himself.[1]

---

*I believe that, early in this century, nicotine remained legal while other drugs were being brought under state control mostly because nicotine allowed people to work, while other drugs attenuated their laboring abilities. (There's a Marxist critique waiting to be developed here by someone.) Its other saving grace, however, is that the "tolerance" that comes with tobacco is not as extreme as that with, say, opiates. Smokers tend to increase their consumption over the first years of smoking, but are able to level out at about 20 cigarettes a day. This contrasts with what we see in some—but by no means all—heroin users: a relatively short cycle of ever-increasing consumption to get the same effect, followed by the terrible crash.

Wartime has provided many of the most vivid instances of tobacco scarcity. Looking back on his experience in World War II, a Mr. N. A. Photiades wrote to the *Times* of London in 1957 to express his doubts about the worth of governmental actions aimed at persuading people to quit smoking. This came days after Britain's Medical Research Council had labeled cigarette smoking a major cause of lung cancer. He wrote:

> I had the misfortune to be a prisoner for nearly four years during the war and found that the one thing that men were unable to give up was cigarette smoking. There was, in fact, a very active market in bartering the handful of rice we received daily for the two cigarettes our hosts so kindly gave us. I have actually seen men die of starvation because they had sold their food for cigarettes. If men under those circumstances cannot abandon smoking, is it likely that we will now—with full pockets and stomachs?[2]

Perhaps the greatest mass example of tobacco deprivation came in Germany after the war, where tobacco was so scarce and so universally valued that it came to serve as a medium of exchange. Someone once told me of an official sign hung in those days over a urinal in a U.S. military bathroom—"Please do not throw cigarette butts in toilets"—and of the note scrawled beneath it: "It makes them soggy and hard to smoke." The serious side to this can be seen in an account of this period written by F. I. Arntzen in 1948:

> Up to a point, the majority of the habitual smokers preferred to do without food even under extreme conditions of nutrition rather than to forgo tobacco. . . . Of 300 German civilians questioned, 256 had obtained tobacco at the black market, 37 had bought tobacco and food, and only 5 had bought food but no tobacco. Many housewives who were smokers bartered fat and sugar for cigarettes. In disregard of considerations of personal dignity, conventional decorum, and esthetic-hygenic feelings, cigarette butts were picked out of the street dirt by people who, on their own statements, would in any other circumstances have felt disgust at such contact. Smokers also condescended to beg for tobacco, but not for other things.[3]

This list could go on, but I think the point is clear: Were tobacco illegal, we would see with it all the depraved trappings of drug culture that we associate with "serious" drugs like heroin or cocaine. Just contemplating such a thing is sobering because of the scale on which tobacco use takes place. There may be 500,000 heroin addicts in this country, but there are nearly 50 million smokers.

CHAPTER **10**

The Threads of Addiction

IN RELATION TO other drugs, tobacco has had, for most of this century, a special status in that it not only has been legal, but has been tolerated in places that are very unlikely sites for the use of drugs, or even alcohol: the workplace, the commuter train, the street. This very status, however, probably has made it in some ways a more difficult drug to give up than the more exotic addictive drugs. That statement may go down a little hard, given the ravages of alcoholism or what we've reviewed regarding the agonies of heroin withdrawal, but we have some interesting evidence on this that falls under our heading, "Ask the experts."

In the 1970s in London, 278 opiate users undergoing treatment at a clinic reported that tobacco was their "most needed" drug, beating out such odds-on favorites as heroin, methadone, and alcohol.[1] In the late 1980s, Lynn Kozlowski and his colleagues at the Addiction Research

Foundation in Toronto posed the following question to a sampling of their patients: "Think of your strongest urge to use cigarettes, and then think of your strongest urge to use alcohol or the drug that brought you here for treatment. Which was stronger?" About two-thirds of the patients reported that their urges for cigarettes were as strong as or stronger than their urges for alcohol. With heroin, about 20 percent reported that their urge to smoke was as strong or stronger than their opiate need.[2]

Even at the lower bound of these studies, think what that means: 20 percent of the Toronto drug abusers had stronger urges to take this *Munchkin* drug tobacco than to use the very archetype of the addictive drug, heroin.

If we ask how this could be so, we have at least a partial explanation at the level of human experience and conditioning. To put the matter simply, drug dependence is inextricably bound up with the setting in which drugs are taken; drug-taking behavior is strengthened to the degree that it is paired with other activities; and no drug on earth is paired with as many activities as is tobacco.

We are in the territory of Pavlov here, but we can use a somewhat more appealing example than his dog to illustrate our point. A woman is invited to dinner at a restaurant she once frequented with her former lover. She has been with someone else for a year now, and she has thought neither of her former lover nor the restaurant in months. But being in the place again, with its familiar lighting and aromas, elicits a profound feeling of loss in her; for a few moments she misses her lover as though she had parted from him yesterday.

Thus with drugs. The importance of the pairing of environment and drug use has been shown in many ways, but we can get an uncluttered look at the process in some animal experiments. To take but one example, in the 1970s Harbans Lal and his colleagues injected a group of lab rats with morphine; each injection was given, however, at the same time that an audible tone was sounded. After several days of this, the tone *by itself* had the power to elicit the physical signs of drug injection in the animals. (The tone raised their rectal temperatures, if you must know, just as morphine did. This may not seem like much of a sign of being high, but it's difficult to get lab rats to express their feelings.) In a different experiment, these researchers made addicts out of another group of rats while pairing a bell sound with morphine injections. They then cut off the supply of morphine, but continued the bell sound for some of the animals. The result? The bell by itself lessened the severity of the narcotic withdrawal these animals were undergoing.[3]

Human beings are not immune to this kind of behavioral conditioning. Former addicts who have long been abstinent from drugs will, like our woman at the restaurant, experience extreme discomfort upon returning to the places in which they abused drugs or underwent withdrawal from them.

Nicotine fits this pattern perfectly. Crucially, no drug of abuse is dosed as often as nicotine, and no drug acts more quickly. Our average smoker "pairs" his experiences with 70,000 hits of nicotine annually, which represents an awesome array of behavioral matchings. Furthermore, it is axiomatic in psychology that the shorter the time between behavior on the one hand and response on the other, the stronger the conditioning effect will be. In this case, the behavior is taking a drag off a cigarette; the response is stimulation, sedation, or any of the other things we've talked about; and the lag time is eight seconds. Whatever else is around with some frequency when this is going on becomes bound up with the smoker's addiction.

What gets attached to the habit? Well, to take one example, there's cigarettes themselves, even if they are unlit. Recall that nicotine usually has the effect of increasing alertness as measured by EEG brain-wave states. Researchers Mangan and Golding found that they could get similar boosts in EEG ratings simply by having smokers "sham smoke" an unlit cigarette while a real one was burning in an ashtray nearby.[4] Smokers who are brought into the laboratory and exposed to smoking "cues," such as the sight of a smoker or tobacco paraphernalia, show increases in heart rate and blood pressure as a result—the very things that happen to them when they actually smoke a cigarette. We even have some reason to believe that the greater this "cue reactivity" is in a smoker, the more difficult he or she is likely to find it to quit smoking.[5]

We can get a more general view of this phenomenon by recalling the Hatsukami and Hughes studies of nicotine withdrawal. Remember that the smokers they studied who underwent abstinence in their regular environment had significantly *more* withdrawal symptoms than the smokers who underwent withdrawal in the isolated setting of the research ward. Withdrawal is worse, in other words, when it touches our everyday experiences.

How does this work in practice? Let's imagine a longtime smoker—say, a poet like W. H. Auden. He gets up and has his first cigarette of the day very quickly to wake himself up. After breakfast, he gets busy writing and has another smoke out of pure physical addiction. The Nag is tugging at him and he must respond or become irritable. He smokes a couple more cigarettes while writing because the nicotine helps him concentrate. He then gets a phone call about 11 A.M. and it's bad news: the IRS is going to audit him in connection with his trip to Italy. He lights a cigarette while he's still on the phone to calm himself down.

Our poet has used tobacco here in four different ways: to alert himself, to satisfy his addiction, to concentrate, and to sedate himself. And he has used it mostly in routine situations; smoking has been paired, in other words, with some of the most basic things in his life. The net that tobacco casts obviously can be rather large, then, but it actually is more extensive than even these examples suggest. Recall that our man smokes his second cigarette of the day because of addiction, which is to say he starts feeling lousy and knows it's time to smoke. Imagine, however, that it's now afternoon and the Nag is *not* calling, but he begins to feel bad because his latest book is not selling well. How does he "interpret" feeling bad? Through thousands of pairings, this feeling has come to mean: it's time to have a cigarette. It will not help with the book sales, but he *reflexively* reaches for the smokes because he has been conditioned to associate dysphoria—of any kind—with the need to smoke. Conversely, if he has learned to associate feeling good with having *had* a cigarette, the net will be further widened in happy situations. (Like sex. There's a notable lack of speculation in the research literature on why the postcoital cigarette appears to be so delicious, but this is one explanation.)

Now let's say our poet decides to quit smoking. He still has trouble getting up in the morning (let's say he did as a child, even before he took up smoking). Now, however, the pick-me-up he turned to every day for 15 years is no longer there. His natural biorhythms, his lifestyle, his work all still point him toward that cigarette, but now he must refuse it. He sits at his desk to write, leans back to consider the scan of a line, and finds himself reaching for the cigarette pack that he habitually kept on the right side of the desk. He will catch himself starting to do this three more times within the hour. Bad news comes his way and he gets halfway through the house looking for a cigarette before he remembers he has quit. Now he has to deal with the bad news *and* the lack of a cigarette. In the evening, he watches television as usual, but there's no pleasure in it. He used to do it while smoking in the most languorous manner, watching the wisps of smoke curl up toward the ceiling, and now all he can think of is that this has become a wretched *half-activity,* along with taking a bath, reading the paper, and any number of other things.

People are tied to smoking as Gulliver was tied to the ground by the Lilliputians: through hundreds of individual threads. Our imagined smoker soon learns that abstinence from nicotine is not a matter of an occasional, abstract longing for a drug. On the contrary, it is the *events* in his life that prompt him to want a cigarette. And not just a few of them, but a profusion: good events, bad events, routine events; you name it.

It should thus be obvious why tobacco makes for an especially virulent addiction. There is a lifestyle that surrounds the use of any drug. But among addictive practices, cigarette smoking is alone in the degree to which public display of it is allowed. (Even alcohol runs a distant second.) The arena in which, say, cocaine addiction is acted out is very narrow—the private room. The arena in which cigarette addiction is acted out is very large, nearly as large as the smoker's life. Thus, whatever power nicotine has becomes multiplied because wherever the tobacco user has set his feet, his environment has included not only common sights and sounds, but a cloud of smoke as well.

CHAPTER **11**

The Personality of Smoking

IN THE VIEW of smoking we've reviewed so far, human beings have been rather like an impressionable surface that can be imprinted with the effects of nicotine and with experience. When you combine the biological effects of nicotine with behavioral conditioning, you get the reasons for smoking. Note that what's implied in this view, however, is a *uniform* surface onto which these things are cast—an unvarying human tabula rasa, if you will.

It's self-evident, I think, that no such thing exists. By the time anyone tries smoking, he or she brings to the act a complex and unique background that will be critically important in determining whether or not the practice will take root. Thus, we can imagine one person who liked the effects of cigarettes, but was put off by the messiness of smoking and so never really took up the habit. Another person liked the effects, but never even thought about the practice being messy, and so took up smoking with avidity.

For someone seeking the causes of smoking, then, the question is not whether people vary in this regard, but whether they vary *by groups*. The question becomes: Does being a Rotarian or a scuba diver make a person more or less likely to be a smoker? This can be helpful because, if we found that all smokers were scuba divers, for example, then that might give us some insight into the rhyme and reason of smoking.

Science essentially is in the business of prediction. (It really is a kind of fortune-telling, though it employs different techniques to achieve this end.) In the area of smoking, it is seeking to be able to make two big predictions, the first of which might be stated: "We predict that if these factors are in place, people will smoke." The second is, "If *these* factors are in place, people will stop." Making such predictions obviously requires more knowledge than we have—it may require more knowledge than we *can* have—but that's the goal, at any rate, and to help us toward it, scientists over the years have asked in any number of ways: Does being in group A make you any more likely to be a smoker than being in group B?

The answer to this clearly is yes. You are more likely (and increasingly likely) to be a smoker if you are poor, for example, or if you are poorly educated. No surprise there. But what about these things: You are more likely to be a smoker if you are divorced; you are far less likely to wear a seat belt if you are a smoker; young white women who smoke are much more likely to be binge drinkers than are their nonsmoking counterparts (almost half are, a rate two to three times higher than that of nonsmoking women); men who are downwardly mobile relative to their parents are more likely to be smokers, while men who are upwardly mobile are less likely.[1]

Some of these things, like the seat belts, might come as no surprise, but others provide more questions than answers. (Being downwardly mobile?) These characteristics are a matter of averages, of course: there are plenty of smokers who wear seat belts and plenty of nonsmokers who don't. Moreover, this does not mean that if you connect these points of information a single smoking "type" will emerge before you. This is a pretty silly idea on the face of it, an old caveat goes, since more than 25 percent of all adult Americans smoke; for there to be a smoking type, one-quarter of all these Americans would have to be a single, recognizable kind of person, which certainly isn't the case.

That said, smokers can be characterized as inordinately *this* or *that* in many ways compared to nonsmokers. This is a bit slippery, since the characteristics of the smoking population change—sometimes at a dramatically rapid rate. In 1968, the percentage of American girls who reported smoking regularly was only half that of American boys; by 1970, the figure was nearly two-thirds; and by January 1974, the percentages were equal.[2]*

Some characteristics associated with smoking are relatively more stable, however, and of these some of the most intriguing have to do with the quality generally called personality.

I think that to the average person, "personality" means about the same thing as vivaciousness; hence, people have "good" personalities to the degree that they can be engaging in public. Stated another way, if a person doesn't "have" much personality, it means he doesn't have much vivaciousness. Thus, in the popular mind, Charo has personality, while Margaret Thatcher does not.

We will be speaking of personality here, however, in a somewhat broader sense. We might take the following as our rough definition of personality: the collection of all those relatively persistent behavioral characteristics that make each person unique. Thus, under this definition, being "disappointed" is not part of a person's personality, but being "easily disappointed" is. There theoretically could be a huge number of such characteristics, but one area of personality psychology, called trait theory, generally holds that there is a relatively small number of important personality characteristics and that these can be measured. Thus, person A may rate a 10 on a 10-point scale that measures hostility, while person B rates only a 5. Since these scales are meant to bear a relation to the real world, one indication of their worth is the *predictive validity* they have. In the example above, we might look at the mile-high hostility rating of person A and predict that he may have done a little time in prison. By such means as checking prediction

---

*Adolescent girls went on to surpass boys in smoking, and their rates remain higher to this day. This has been an important part of a notable shift in smoking patterns in the United States. If current long-term trends hold, sometime in the 1990s the United States will achieve the dubious distinction of being first nation I am aware of in the history of the planet to have more female than male smokers.

against fact, the more sophisticated personality scales (or the larger "inventories") have come to be fine-tuned to the point that most psychologists would agree that they are measuring something real.

Any number of personality traits have been tested to see what correlations turn up with smoking. The question being asked here is: Do smokers distinctively share any personality traits when we compare them to nonsmokers?

The answer is yes. Any list of these traits is somewhat arbitrary by necessity; evidence for them can balance the results from many studies, and there is no litmus test for a "proven" correlation. Also, it's important to note that these characteristics don't account for much of the "variance" in smoking; knowing that a person has a given personality trait will not allow us to predict with any confidence whether he or she is a smoker.

Still, these associations definitely do give us some insight, I believe, into smoking. We might begin by looking at some traits that we wouldn't find too surprising in smokers. As a group, they tend to rank higher than nonsmokers on scales that measure what is called risk-taking and sensation-seeking. People who score high on these scales might also be found in the ranks of sky divers, white-water rafters, or the takers of other drugs. (Or, I would guess, policemen, an inordinate number of whom, it seems to me, are smokers.)

The reasons for smokers' disproportionate representation in these groups seem self-evident: smoking is a risk and smoking provides a whole constellation of physical and mental sensations.

Related to risk-taking is another personality correlation found in smokers: they rate high on what is called an "external control" scale. That is, relative to nonsmokers, they tend to see their fortunes as being controlled by forces outside of them—by other people or fate—rather than by forces inside them. As researcher Gene Smith put it, "Smokers are more likely than nonsmokers to think that what happens to them is due more to chance than to their own efforts and skills."[3] No great surprise here, either. For all our medical advances, lung cancer and heart disease still are like slots on a roulette wheel. Do our actions matter much in making the ball stop on red or black? A disproportionate number of smokers would say no. This notion of external control is obviously congruent, as well, with our observation about risk-taking.

Smokers tend to rank high in a constellation of characteristics that collectively are referred to in the now quaintly old-fashioned term "antisocial." This means that, among other things, they tend to be more rebellious, be more defiant, and have higher levels of misconduct. The correlations in this category are very strong, and they are complemented by the finding that smokers tend to rank *lower* in the personality category of deference.

Beyond this, smokers seem to have what can only be called a higher sex drive—or perhaps a lower sex inhibition—than do nonsmokers. The studies are few in number here, but nearly all of them point in the same direction, measuring such things as sexual precociousness, the "need" for sex, and attraction to the opposite sex, and taking this measure among such diverse groups as U.S. adult males and undergraduates at a Catholic women's college in the northeast.

To continue with this picture, smokers rank high in impulsiveness; relative to nonsmokers, they tend to make snap judgments. Finally, we have reason to believe that smokers are more honest than nonsmokers in the view of themselves that they present to others. Most personality inventories contain a "lie" scale that is intended to give those evaluating the test a sense of how candid the test taker has been. (The items on this scale usually are a series of statements scattered throughout, such as, "I do not always tell the truth," or "I am sometimes cold to my spouse." If a test taker consistently denies having these everyday failings, it is unlikely that he or she is being truthful in general.) The studies we have on this indicate that smokers are less likely to lie on such tests; one theory has it that their lack of deference and their surfeit of defiance combine to make them relatively indifferent to what people think of them.

A subject that invariably comes up in any discussion of smoking and personality has to do with a trait that is so broad and variously defined that researchers have trouble even agreeing on a name for it. It is sometimes referred to as "mental health," sometimes as "emotionality," and sometimes as "neuroticism." (Hence one influential scale refers to it by the shorthand "N"—as in "those who have high N.") Those who do have high N are generally nervous, overwrought, and hyperreactive to the world around them. They are anxious, restless, pessimistic. The opposite side of this coin is being stable, which means being calm, steady, even-tempered. In a bit of language that could have come out of *Monty Python*, these stable folk are sometimes referred to in the literature as "normals."

The question is whether smokers as a group have higher N than nonsmokers. In Gene Smith's comprehensive early survey, slightly more than half of all the 50-odd studies conducted showed a relationship between smoking and some aspect of this group of characteristics. In all instances where a relationship was found, smokers had poorer mental health than nonsmokers, but the fact that nearly half the experiments found no significant relationship ought to give us pause. Since that time, additional surveys have been conducted, most of them giving smokers a higher N rating than nonsmokers. As it turns out, however, this may be more true of *women* smokers than of smokers in general.[4]

These findings about mental health have been considerably sharpened, in a sense, with a series of studies in recent years on the connection between smoking and a very specific mental affliction: depression.

In 1986, John Hughes and his colleagues examined a group of psychiatric outpatients in Minnesota and found that more than half of them smoked, a figure that is, of course, way above the national average.[5] About half of these smokers, it turned out, suffered from an affliction that is known as major depressive disorder. This is not the everyday blue mood that most of us are subject to from time to time, but a debilitating condition, often appearing in the form of identifiable "episodes," that can leave its victims unable to function for weeks or even months at a time.

Then, in 1988, Alexander Glassman and his co-workers, who were doing a stop-smoking experiment, found to their surprise that more than 60 percent of the heavy smokers they were studying had a history of this same kind of major depression.[6] Glassman's subjects were not psychiatric outpatients, as in the Hughes study, but people brought together only because they shared the trait of being heavy smokers who wanted to quit. Since major depression is thought to occur in less than 10 percent of the general population, the proportion of depressives in Glassman's group—six times the national rate—prompted him to call for some work that might confirm his findings.

That work was eventually done in part by Glassman himself; it came to light in 1990 with the publication of two papers in the *Journal of the American Medical Association.* In one of them, Glassman and his colleagues reported on information they had assembled on more than 3,200 people who had been interviewed in the St. Louis area. What they found fully confirmed their earlier suspicions: people with this serious depressive disorder are more likely to smoke and they find it much more difficult to stop smoking.[7]

Right next to Glassman's paper was one by Robert Anda and his co-workers, who studied data collected on 820 people from across the United States. Anda looked at persons who suffered from chronic depression (without the "major" in front of it). This is a serious, persistent mental affliction, but it is not necessarily as profound a condition as the depression Glassman studied. What Anda and his co-workers found was that about 20 percent of the smokers they studied rated high on a depression scale. Furthermore, these smokers were 40 percent less likely to have quit than nondepressed smokers.[8]

With this work, the link between smoking and a spectrum of depression seems securely identified. What has not been nailed down is whether chronic depression is a factor in making people *take up* smoking, but we have reason to believe that, with adolescents, the more depressed they are, the more likely it is they will start to smoke.

What can we make of the somewhat equivocal evidence linking neuroticism to smoking and the strong evidence linking depression to it? We've seen that nicotine may be able to act as a kind of all-purpose psychological tool. It should not be surprising, then, that those who are more troubled mentally would be more inclined to turn to it for assistance. We have some reason to believe that more neurotic smokers take bigger, deeper drags; this would be consistent with smoking for a calming effect, which makes sense. Certainly it is consistent with the popular image of an overwrought smoker taking big drags as if the cigarette were a lifeline to sanity.

Lest it pass by unnoticed, however, what this evidence suggests is that, for some people, smoking may be a form of *self-medication,* as the research literature phrases it. That is, it may be a pharmacological aid—medicine—to people who have a preexisting mental affliction such as neuroticism or depression.

My response to this is: Say it isn't so. Is it not perverse that perhaps 10 million troubled Americans should be made to feel better—to feel "normal," actually—by taking a drug that provides its comfort only by supplying addiction and death in the bargain? Here in our indifferent universe, this may well be the case.

Where does this leave us with respect to advising these people to stop smoking? For those who suffer only from mild, infrequent bouts of depression, the advice probably would remain the same: quit. But what about those who suffer from debilitating, lengthy, and frequent attacks of depression? Glassman has reported that heavily depressed smokers who are able to quit seem to be at increased risk of plunging into a new depressive episode. It is possible, of course, that what is depressing these people is simple nicotine withdrawal. But if their depression does stem from the fact that they have lost their medicine, then would we advise them to preserve their lungs and heart at the cost of sacrificing their day-to-day peace of mind?

Depression is only one form of mental affliction, of course, and as a result of the kind of work we've been discussing, science is beginning to identify more precisely the mental dysfunctions that are linked to smoking. In his study, Glassman found that the psychiatric conditions of phobia, panic, or obsessive-compulsive disorder were *not* independently related to smoking. On the other hand, in his study of the psychiatric outpatients, Hughes found a whopping 88 percent smoking rate among the schizophrenics he studied.

This last statistic came as no surprise to me, and I doubt that any reader is much fazed by it either. From simple observation, I would have guessed that there is a 100 percent smoking rate among the ranks of America's schizophrenics, if those who are out on the streets are any indication. I feel certain that, at the end of the day, we will find that smoking *is* a form of self-medication for these grossly disturbed people.* What we can hope is that for these poor souls—and for others who may be turning to nicotine as medicine—science can someday

---

*The connection between smoking and mental illness is not something that's just recently been discovered; for that matter, the connection between smoking and many types of proscribed behavior seems to have a long history. Writing 100 years ago, Tolstoy could ask: "Why do gamblers almost all smoke? Why among women do those who lead a regular life smoke least? Why do prostitutes and madmen *all* smoke?"[9] Why indeed?

produce substances that can offer the help and attractiveness of tobacco without its perverse side effects.

We have one final personality category to consider that deserves attention from us and it is, readers may be glad to know, a lighter topic than the one we've been looking at. The category is extroversion/introversion, and it needs to be studied in the context of the person responsible for most of the seminal research linking it to smoking, H. J. Eysenck.

Hans Jurgen Eysenck is perhaps the best known psychologist in Britain and certainly one of the most influential psychologists in the world in the area of personality theory. The breadth of his work has extended well beyond the world of academic psychology, however. Eysenck is an intellectual gadfly of sorts, having managed to tweak the noses of diverse sections of the thinking world in a prolific career that now spans more than 40 years. He has had the impertinence to suggest, for example, that the emperor Freud has no clothes, that astrology may have some value, and that those who stand on the political far right and the far left have a great deal in common psychologically.*

Much of this work, however, has been a kind of spin-off from the core of his academic research on personality. In Eysenck's view, introversion/extroversion is not a mere personality trait, but, along with neuroticism/stability and psychoticism/superego, a crucial "dimension" of personality.

The definitions Eysenck uses for introversion and extroversion are pretty much those of the layman. Thus the typical introvert

> is a quiet, retiring sort of person, introspective, fond of books rather than people; he is reserved and reticent except with intimate friends. He tends to plan ahead, "looks before he leaps" and distrusts the impulse of the moment. He does not like excitement, takes matters of everyday life with proper seriousness and likes a well ordered mode of life. He keeps his feelings under close control, seldom behaves in an aggressive manner and does not lose his temper easily.[10]

---

*Some of these positions have received more support than others. Eysenck has championed the view, for example, that tobacco's causal role in disease has never been proved, a position that almost no one outside the tobacco industry takes seriously.

While the extrovert

is sociable, likes parties, has many friends, needs to have people to talk
to. . . . He craves excitement, takes chances, acts on the spur of the
moment and is generally an impulsive individual. He is fond of
practical jokes, always has a ready answer and generally likes change;
he is carefree, easy-going, optimistic and likes to "laugh and be
merry." He prefers to keep moving and doing things, tends to be
aggressive and loses his temper quickly; his feelings are not kept under
tight control and he is not always a reliable person.[11]

Introversion and extroversion are not all-or-nothing qualities. Most
people are "ambiverts," falling into a middle range that is neither highly
introverted nor highly extroverted. Moreover, just as sports teams are
made up of individual players, so introversion and extroversion actually
are made up of individual traits whose interaction defines the broader
characteristic.

Keeping this in mind, it's worth noting the kind of *behaviors* that
are correlated with one's place on the introversion-extroversion scale.
Extroverts change jobs, houses, and spouses more than introverts do;
they are more active sexually, doing it earlier, with more partners, in
more positions, for longer periods of time, and in kinkier ways; they
drink more alcohol and more coffee, prefer spicier foods more frequently, take more risks, and have more car accidents than do introverts.[12]
They are also more easily distracted and concentrate less well on boring
or repetitive tasks.

Introversion and extroversion have a basis in biology, it turns out.
In Eysenck's original formulation, introverts had a higher "resting" state
of brain arousal—their brains idled at a higher rate than extroverts, we
might say. This has turned out not to be the case, but what is true is that
introverts and extroverts *respond* much differently to the world they
encounter.

Put an introvert in an experiment booth side by side with an
extrovert and give each of them a moderate auditory signal, and the
introvert's brain will react much more strongly than will the
extrovert's—it responds with a higher level of activity. The same is true
when the stimulus is visual, rather than auditory. (These things are

measured both by brain responses and by skin conductance responses, or the degree to which electricity travels across the skin.) What introverts have is not a higher level of *resting arousal* than extroverts, but rather a higher level of *arousability*.[13] They are more aroused by the stimuli they receive from their environment.

This has implications for how these two groups of people perceive their world and interact with it. Introverts have a lower tolerance to pain than do extroverts, whether it's low intensity or high intensity. Meanwhile, as Eysenck has reported, extroverts are less tolerant of sensory deprivation than are introverts. Extroverts actually prefer more intense auditory stimulation than do introverts.[14]

All this relates to the concept of an optimal "hedonic tone" for human beings. It's probably self-evident that none of us likes too much or too little stimulation. In the extremes, few people would choose to spend much time floating in a sensory-deprivation tank or standing around a jackhammer. The level of arousal we would experience in either state is simply uncomfortable to us. How would we expect this fact to affect introverts and extroverts? Well, an optimal state of arousal for the average person could well be a state of *underarousal* for an extrovert and a state of *overarousal* for an introvert. Why? The extrovert's brain is experiencing incoming stimulation more weakly than is the average person's—because of his low state of arousability— while the introvert is experiencing this stimulation more strongly.

This is summed up nicely by Eysenck, who says that extroverts exist in a condition that amounts to a "stimulus hunger." Thus, we might not be surprised that extroverts eat more spicy food, drink more alcohol, change jobs and lovers more frequently, and the rest, because each of these things is an activity that provides stimulation in abundance. (Professional and amateur athletes, by the way, tend to be extroverts, which makes sense along all the lines we've talked about.)[15]

Now, if readers will indulge me for a second, I cannot resist making a few cultural observations about all this, though these things have nothing to do with our essential story. First, given the broad acceptance of the work on this topic, it's something of a surprise to me that knowledge of these introvert/extrovert differences has not entered the domain of popular received wisdom, along with right-brain/left-brain, Freudian slip, and the like.

Second, I think it might be good if this *did* happen, since it's my impression that a lot of extroverts, extreme and mild, are walking around with a false conceit: that introverts are a bit *dull* mentally. To put it another way, there is a feeling, in society in general, I think, that the sign of an active brain is an active tongue. As we have seen, if any group can lay claim to being mentally sluggish, it is extroverts, not introverts (who do better at school, incidentally.)

Finally, should these things become generally known, I think it could lead to a whole new class of discriminatory jokes, such as: Did you hear about the introvert who put on a shocking pink sweatshirt? He passed out from the overload. Or: Why do extroverts eat such spicy food? So they can stay awake until dessert.

But our question here is: Do introversion and extroversion tell us anything about smoking? Well, we have evidence that introverts and extroverts are pulled in different directions by nicotine—and, for that matter, by caffeine—and that these directions are precisely those that we would predict might be attractive to members of both groups.

To illustrate: Barry Smith and his colleagues measured the skin responses of a group of extroverts and a group of introverts, dosing both groups with identical amounts of caffeine while subjecting them to auditory tones. As expected, the introverts reacted more strongly to the tones when they listened to them in a placebo (no-caffeine) condition. The interesting thing was that, as the introverted subjects received caffeine, they became less responsive to the tones; the more caffeine they got, the less responsive they became. The reaction of the extroverts, however, was the exact opposite: the more caffeine they got, the *more* strongly they reacted to the sounds they were hearing.[16]

This opposite-reaction phenomenon has been documented with nicotine as well, through observation of a brain wave we discussed earlier, the contingent negative variation (CNV). (This is the wave evoked during the period between an alerting command, such as "ready," and an action command, such as "go.") As Kieron O'Connor and others have reported, nicotine increases the CNV magnitude for extroverts, but decreases it for introverts.[17]

Why this should be so isn't clear, but these effects are precisely what we might predict both introverts and extroverts would want: Our underaroused extroverts are upping their reaction levels with caffeine or nicotine, while our overaroused introverts are bringing their reaction levels down.

We have reason to believe this phenomenon means something out in the real world. William Revelle and his colleagues at Northwestern University have found that extroverts are helped in carrying out complex tasks when they are given doses of caffeine in the morning equal to several cups of coffee, while introverts are hindered by the drug.[18]

With all of this, we might guess that extroverts and introverts would be equally attracted to smoking—one group stimulating itself and the other group dampening itself as desired. But this turns out not to be the case. As it happens, smokers are inordinately extroverted. This is perhaps the most robust personality correlation in all the literature. In 1970, Gene Smith found 22 of 25 analyses reporting that smokers were more extroverted, and there have been very few contrary studies in the years since then. These differences are not large—extroversion doesn't account for much of the "variance" in smoking—and there are plenty of introverted smokers, but the differences are consistent. Furthermore, the more a person smokes, the more extroverted he or she is likely to be. Light smokers are the least extroverted, heavy smokers the most, but all groups of smokers are more extroverted than are nonsmokers. (Actually, all groups of *cigarette* smokers are more extroverted; we find pipe smokers exactly where we would guess they would end up on this scale: at the most introverted point, even more introverted than nonsmokers.)

So why are smokers more extroverted? Even without the biological information we've reviewed, we might have guessed that extroverts would be disproportionately attracted to smoking. After all, there is a large element of public display in extroversion, and smoking—with its strange object and huge clouds of smoke—means the smoker will be something of a cynosure wherever he goes.

But is there a biological reason for the oversupply of extroverts among smokers? Well, one could guess that the *act* of smoking provides more rewards for extroverts than for introverts. We observed early on that anyone seeking stimulation has come to the right place with cigarettes, since they seem to offer a bit of everything: sights, sounds, smells, tastes. It wouldn't be any surprise, then, if sensation-seeking extroverts were differentially attracted to this extremely sensual practice. In this view, odd as it may seem, the reward of smoking for these people would be similar to the reward of basketball or the reward of sex.

More elaborate explanations have been put forward regarding the surfeit of extroverted smokers, but in my view they are so difficult *and* speculative that, for our purposes, the understanding gained may not be worth the explanation.

We noted earlier that the characteristics of the smoking population change over time; in the past few years, we've seen a sea-change in smoking by way of the dramatic reduction of the number of people who do it. Smoking's reduced acceptability may also mean a change in the kind of personality correlations that are observed. Eysenck has written of how extroverts increasingly may have a motive *not* to smoke, given the stigma society has attached now to the practice.[19] Conversely, we may see smoking's correlations with antisocial tendencies increase if this process goes on.

My own feeling, however, is that there is some component of extroversion that will continue to correlate very strongly with smoking—more strongly than the current data on extroversion per se would indicate. Readers may have noticed that many of the traits associated with extroversion—impulsiveness, risk taking, sexuality—are the same as the individual correlations found with smoking. In this general personality dimension, it seems to me, there is quite a strong link with smoking. In a scientific spirit, I would like to invite readers to demonstrate this to themselves by performing the following experiment. Arrange to go to a relaxed gathering of actors, rock musicians, or hairdressers on the one hand, or civil engineers, electricians, or computer programmers on the other, and observe how much smoking is going on. If your experience is anything like mine, the differences should be dramatic.

• • •

To take a broader view of this topic of personality, the spirit of our era dictates that we should debunk stereotypes wherever we find them, but in the case of smoking and personality, it seems to me that our stereotypes have a great deal of validity to them. We have observed that it is misleading to *connect* various smoking-and-personality associations and thus come up with a putative smoking "type." Fair enough, but it seems to me remarkable how good the fit is between the personality correlations we've reviewed and society's image of the smoker. We can get a clear picture of this when we look at fictive characters whose smoking is emblematic of them.

Restless, defiant, risk-taking, highly sexed, abrasively honest: Is this out of a psychology text, or is it a description of Humphrey Bogart in *The Maltese Falcon?* Impulsive, undeferential, depressed, and sensation-seeking: Is this a portrait of a smoker, or of James Dean in *Rebel Without a Cause?* Sexually driven, fast living, risk-taking: Do we have smoking correlations here or descriptions of William Hurt and Kathleen Turner in *Body Heat?* If it's true that few smokers are *all* these things, it is equally true that smokers tend to be *some* of these things more often than do nonsmokers. Society has turned a pretty sensitive ear to these interconnections, it seems to me, and we see a distillation of these perceptions in these characters.

When these personality traits are looked at in overview, the overarching image of smokers I am left with is of people who want *more* (just like extroverts) and are willing to travel some dangerous routes to get it. Appropriately enough—as if life were a script written for a movie—a good number of these people pay the price for trying to fly so close to the sun. This is true not only on the statistical level, but on the personal level as well. James Dean died in a car wreck, Humphrey Bogart of throat cancer.

To put it another way, however, smokers seem inordinately *driven* in a way that nonsmokers are not. To my way of thinking, this extends beyond the wild-side areas we've talked about and into more acceptable arenas, such as work and achievement. If we look statistically at the *whole* of the smoking population, this is certainly not the case: smokers do worse in school, get in trouble more often, make less money, and all the rest. I suspect, however, that if we drew up some arbitrary list of high achievers in America we would find a surprisingly *high* proportion of smokers. (Or former smokers; this effect would be expected to fade with the waning of smoking.) Who has been a smoker? How about Robert Bork, William Bennett, James Baker, Dick Cheney, Connie Chung, Ted Koppel, Jeffrey Katzenberg, Bartlett Giamatti, Jack Nicholson, Joan Didion, Garrison Keillor, Jacqueline Onassis, Alexander Haig, Leonard Bernstein, Bob Fosse, Sarah Vaughan, Joni Mitchell, Helen Frankenthaler, Robert Noyce, and Mike Nichols, just for starters. My guess is that the yearning to achieve and to be something runs hand-in-hand with the yearning to feel and do.

Finally, it may be futile for social scientists to try to squelch notions of a smoking "type," because there is an industry in this country that reinforces such notions every day on a massive scale. In advertising, we find an institution that has connected the points of information about smoking and personality—much as one would in a dot-to-dot picture—to give us full-color portraits of a smoking type. We can pick two particularly sterling examples of this in the Camel Filters Guy and the Virginia Slims Gal. Think of him first, all by himself out on safari with only a Coleman lantern to keep him company. Risk-taking? You bet. Defiant, sensation-seeking, sexy, disturbingly honest? Of course. And her? Extroverted, impulsive, sensation-seeking, and sexy from her hair to her shoes? You've got it. These images should give us a good deal more faith in what academic research has told us about smoking and personality. The double-breasted marketing researchers seem to have come up with the same answers as the tweedy academic types.

CHAPTER 12

The Motivation That Precedes Us

In THE SAME way that acetate transparencies can be overlaid onto maps to show additional features of a piece of terrain, we have overlaid the concepts of behavioral conditioning and personality onto our description of smoking to give ourselves a more complete view of the practice. We will now carry out that procedure once again with a final concept before bringing our inquiry on smoking motivation to a close.

The motivational factor we will examine is different from all the others we've talked about because it has no component of human volition to it. (Even our dark-world concept of drug addiction leaves room for human choice.) We will look here at the motivation that is present before we are fully formed as human beings, the motivation that precedes us, if you will—genetics.

What we are talking about is the idea that smoking is to some degree heritable, in the same way that having blue eyes is. The question is whether or not the genetic makeup of some human beings predisposes them to take up or stay with the practice of smoking.

Smoking researchers generally agree that this is the case. Furthermore, the degree to which this is true is loosely agreed upon as well.

Common sense tells us that this genetic influence cannot be overwhelming. In 1964, 53 percent of the men in the United States smoked, compared to 32 percent of the women.[1] As we have seen, however, in the 1990s, there may be more women than men smoking in this country. The genetic makeup of American men and women has not changed much since 1964; what has changed is the fit between smoking and what it means to be a man or a woman in the United States. Womanliness is now less threatened by smoking, and manliness is perhaps less aided by it.

That said, genetics is acknowledged to play a role in the adoption and maintenance of the smoking habit. How do we know? How can we tease out the influence of upbringing on the one hand from that of genetics on the other? There are several time-honored practices for trying to differentiate the contribution of nurture from that of nature, but among the most common are adoption and twin studies.

Though these studies can be terribly complex in their details—the math here can get pretty sophisticated—their outline is simple. In adoption studies, scientists look at a given behavior, like smoking, and ask: Is the behavior of an adopted child more like that of his biological parents or more like that of his adoptive parents?

In twin studies, the question is: Are twins more alike in this behavior than are other siblings? Specifically, are monozygotic (MZ) twins more alike in the behavior than dizygotic (DZ) twins? Having developed from a single egg, monozygotic (identical) twins have an identical genetic makeup, while dizygotic (fraternal) twins are no more alike genetically than are nontwin brothers and sisters. The question here is: When MZ twins are raised together, are they more like each other in terms of smoking behavior than are DZ twins raised together? (As scientists would put it, is their behavior more concordant?) Some muddying of the nature/nurture contributions can occur even in this instance, however, in that identical twins may be *treated* more alike than fraternal twins are. (Since identical twins are always of the same sex, while fraternal twins are not, this is a distinct possibility.) Therefore, a variation on this technique is to study the concordance rates of MZ twins reared *apart* in relation to DZ twins reared apart.

If we find that MZ twins have greater concordance rates than DZ twins, then this represents strong evidence that the behavior in question is under some genetic influence. The greater the difference in concordance between MZ and DZ twins, the greater the assumed degree of genetic control. The reasoning behind this probably is self-evident. One group of twins has identical genes but completely different environments; nevertheless, they end up sharing some behavior or trait—smoking, *not* smoking, drinking, obesity—to a greater extent than do twins who don't have the same genes. What is "driving" the identical twins toward this shared behavior? The assumption is that they are predisposed to it by their genes.

One early piece of research on genetic influence can give us an idea of the kinds of results we're talking about. In 1962 James Shields looked at the smoking status of 42 pairs of MZ twins reared apart. Of these 42 pairs, only 9 were discordant—one of the twins being a smoker while the other was not. Conversely, 18 pairs were both nonsmokers—they were concordant for not smoking—and 15 were both smokers. Contrast this with what we would expect by chance: 21 should have been discordant rather than 9; 12 should have been concordant for not smoking rather than 18; and 9 should have been concordant for smoking rather than 15. As it turns out, the odds of this happening by chance are less than one in a thousand.[2]

We have more confidence in such figures, however, if we see them replicated in a large number of studies. John Hughes reported on reviews of 18 "reared together" twin studies and found that concordance rates for smoking were consistently higher in MZ than in DZ twins. Further, two of three "reared apart" studies in addition to Shields's work reveal that concordance rates for MZ twins are greater than those for DZ twins.[3]

The question then becomes: How much greater? According to Hughes, only a modest amount: the magnitude of the increase in concordance is usually about 5 to 15 percent.

The only adoption study we have on the topic—done by Hans Eysenck with geneticist L. J. Eaves—showed that the amount of smoking of adoptees was correlated with the amount their biologic parents smoked, but not correlated at all with how much their adoptive parents smoked. Here again, then, we have evidence of some genetic influence, but here again the amount of influence did not seem particularly great, since it came out only slightly in excess of what science deems statistically significant.[4]

Still, these differences do lead in some interesting directions. One team of Australian researchers found that Australian MZ twins had consistent, significantly higher correlations not only for taking up smoking, but for what they called "committed smoking," arbitrarily defined as being a current smoker who has been smoking for at least 10 years.

Now, we have reason to believe that women have a harder time giving up smoking than do men. This issue isn't settled, as the data on it are competing, but we do know that the percentage of *former* male smokers in the United States has increased to a greater extent than the percentage of former female smokers among those who are 50 years old or more.[5]

Consistent with this, the Australian researchers found a higher prevalence of ex-smokers among older men than among older women. Several theories have been put forth as to why a phenomenon like this might take place, but the Australians offer a genetic hypothesis. In, say, the 1950s, the societal pressures not to smoke would have been stronger on women than on men. Therefore, among women who *did* take up smoking, we might expect a higher proportion to have been genetically disposed to do so. In the 1980s, when societal pressures were on *not* to smoke, a higher proportion of men would be able to quit than women, because a smaller proportion of the male smoking population would be *genetically* disposed to smoke.[6] Put another way, as a group, older women smokers have a proportionately larger core of genetically driven smokers, and these people would have more trouble quitting smoking than would environmentally driven smokers, who are disproportionately male.

The whole question of genetics and drug abuse is a touchy one, of course, because to the degree that genes do play a role in such behavior, drug abuse might be thought of as a disease—inheritable like, say, Huntington's chorea—which accordingly would lessen the amount of responsibility drug takers have for their act.

We need to consider what this means, however, in light of what we know about genetics and smoking. To recycle a formulation we've used before, to say *that* genes exercise some control over smoking behavior is not to say *how* they exercise this control. We have here another instance of human beings being a black box: we look at what goes in one side (the genes of parents), and we know what comes out the other (some genetic influence over smoking), but we need to ask: How is this being put into effect *inside?* Sad to relate, on this issue, the black box of the human being is shut very tightly.

To understand why, we need to appreciate the essence of what genes do. The task of genes is to direct the production of a group of chemical workers in the body called enzymes (or proteins). A gene is simply a length of DNA that "codes" for the production of an enzyme. This enzyme, having been created, then proceeds to do some work by aiding in more chemical reactions in the body. In the classic representation of this process—now somewhat outdated—a single gene will create a single enzyme that has a very specific task, such as helping create red blood cells or repairing skin tissue or any number of other things. Under this view, a gene is rather like a straw boss who says, "Give me some of A, some of B, and some of C . . ." and so on for thousands of steps. When all these chemicals have been put together, an enzyme is created that gets busy on some task.

From this account, it may be apparent that we do not have a gene in our bodies that creates an enzyme which opens a cigarette package, pulls out a fag, lights the thing up, and so forth. It must be that genetic influence is operating at some higher level of biological organization than the one-gene/one-enzyme model we've looked at. The body's liver, for example, represents a collection of many different kinds of cells that work together to create a functioning *system,* and it is to one (or more) of these systems that we would probably have to look for the genetic locus of control of smoking. When we review the smoking research literature on what systems might be involved, however, we find only a couple of candidates, and each of these has a high degree of speculation attached to it.

Hans Eysenck has put forward the idea that gene influence is mediated in part through personality. He and other researchers have produced a large body of work indicating that genes strongly shape major personality characteristics. How strongly? Based on twin studies and other data, a consensus seems to be emerging among these scientists that genes account for about 50 percent of personality.[7] (Though I hasten to add that conclusions such as these about genetics are strongly disputed by other scientists.)

Well, where might this genetic effect take place in the body? In other words, what physical *system* might be involved that would allow genes to help shape personality? We have observed that introverts have higher levels of arousability than do extroverts. And we've also seen that general arousal states are most strongly controlled by an area of our brain stem called the reticular formation. Might it be that the arousal strength generated by this system differs between introverts and extroverts? If so, we would expect that introverts and extroverts would differ in some inherited gene that would differentially affect their reticular formations. Is this the case? No one has a clue. In other words, speculation about a rather high level of physical organization (the reticular formation) is about as detailed as we can get as to how genes might affect personality, which in turn seems to affect smoking.

Even if this mechanism is in place, however, it may not mean that much because, as we've seen, personality doesn't seem to affect smoking *that much*. For such genetic control over smoking as there is, we might have to look toward other mechanisms *in addition to* personality. How about genetic differences in the medial forebrain bundle? How about genetic differences in metabolism? How about genetically sensitive lips?*

The point is clear, I suppose: there are any number of other systems we could think of that might affect smoking, but we're absolutely in the dark as to what they may be. So far as the *how* of genetics and smoking goes, the black box is closed very tightly indeed.

This question of genes and drug abuse is a matter of more than academic interest, since it might have some bearing on how the smoker

---

*Genetic effects do not all take place within the body. As Thomas Bouchard, Jr., and his colleagues have pointed out, a young child who is active is likely to be treated differently by his parents than one who is sedentary. To the degree that the child's activity level is genetically driven, genes influence his environment—and his environment in turn influences him further. This is but one example of a gene-environment "covariance," which is a likely mechanism for explaining how genes help shape the person.[8]

who is trying to quit views his or her condition. The question might go: Who's in control here, me or my genes? Given our present level of knowledge about genetics and smoking, the answer I would give is: Who cares? The *behavior* that's going to have to be exhibited to quit smoking is the same—though the intensity of effort required may vary—no matter what power genetics has. Knowledge that genes exercise some modest amount of influence over smoking could, just possibly, be of assistance, in that a person might assume he or she is of a genetically determined "type" and develop a rock-sure belief that permanent, total abstinence is the only kind of quitting that's likely to be effective—which is probably true. On the other hand, such a belief could just as easily cut the other way and result in a person's becoming a resigned smoker.

The point I'm trying to get at is that concern among the general populace about genes and drug abuse really serves little practical purpose. Conversely, scientists have very good reasons for pursuing this knowledge in hopes that we might someday accumulate enough information to be of value. As John Hughes has pointed out, we have a glimmer of practicality on the genetic front with the notion of identifying children who are likely to be most at risk for becoming smokers. (Family studies hold some promise in this area.) Until such time as we are vastly more informed about genes and drug use, however, it seems to me that people might as well act as if their destiny rests fully with themselves and not with their stars.

CHAPTER 13

In and Out of Dracula's Lair

But oh, what witchcraft of a stronger kind
Or cause too deep for human search to find,
Makes earth-born weeds imperial man enslave—
Not little souls, but e'en the wise and brave!
—17TH-CENTURY POEM, FROM ARBUCKLE

WHY DO PEOPLE smoke cigarettes? At the risk of belaboring the obvious, the account that I have given here assumes that people smoke for all the reasons we have reviewed. Not all smokers will be motivated by every factor we've looked at, but all of them will be affected by some of these things. We have thus pursued a line of inductive reasoning, going from particular motivations—genes, behavioral conditioning, biological reward—to arrive at a general, seemingly innocuous conclusion: People smoke for a great variety of reasons, each of which contributes some increment of motivation to the practice. Added together, these motivations are enough to make people stay with this destructive, goofy habit.

A crucial phrase here, however, is "stay with" the habit. It should be obvious that whatever benefits nicotine may provide, it cannot deliver them until the smoker's first cigarette has been lit up. We have only touched on a few of the reasons that people—adolescents and very young adults, really—light up that first fag. In this same vein, we have hardly touched smoking's other bookend: why some smokers who are trying to quit relapse while others are able to achieve abstinence (though this subject is covered to some extent in the appendix). While these are extremely important topics, I have chosen not to pursue them because they amount to intellectual domains unto themselves, and what we have looked at apart from them is weighty enough.

The gist of what I have put forward as to why people smoke is notable in that it contains no overarching theory of smoking motivation—no theory, at any rate, that goes beyond what I said at the outset: that people smoke primarily to get nicotine into their bodies. Once nicotine starts circulating in the human bloodstream there are as many reactions to it, I would say, as there are people who ingest it. Any theory that can encompass this diversity is a theory we probably can do without.

We could leave it at that except for one thing. What we have learned about smoking motivation seems applicable to several overarching theories of drug use that *do* exist and that have some currency in society. I would like to use what smoking tells us to add my two cents worth to this discussion. In turn, looking at these theories stands to help inform our view of smoking. Finally, all this can be applied to ideas about social policy in relation to drug use.

We have used the term "addiction" in this book to refer to the *sum* of all those things that go into creating the compulsive behavior of smoking. Thus, addiction has included, for example, components of physical dependence, behavioral conditioning, and the desire to retain the performance enhancements that nicotine seems able to provide.

As we noted at the outset, this view of addiction stands in distinction to the way the average person looks at drug addiction (some carrot, a lot of stick). To be somewhat broader about it than we were at the start, if Americans stopped to think about it, they would realize that they really have two models in their head concerning addiction. One involves alcohol, the other involves drugs like heroin.

The alcoholism model is actually the alcoholism *disease* model, and it goes something like this: Most people can take or leave alcohol as they please, but a small minority of drinkers is predisposed to the disease of alcoholism, much as a small minority of people is predisposed to early heart attacks. Once people in this susceptible group start drinking, they are certain to become alcoholics because they cannot control themselves in connection with their drinking.

The heroin contact model is a little different. It holds that *anyone* who comes in contact with heroin often enough will become an addict. No "disease" is required here; the drug itself is potent enough, this view holds, to make anyone who uses it frequently dependent on it to the point of addiction. Once a person reaches this status of "addict," this view holds, he is permanently prone to relapse into heroin use, as if he had once contracted malaria and now were susceptible to recurrences of it. We could probably fit crack cocaine, certain opiate-like prescription drugs, and nicotine into this model as well.

There is another theory, however, that has been coalescing through the work of some writers and researchers that wisely, in my view, rejects these notions and puts in their place the following ideas. First, all addictions can fall under a great deal of human control, and it is worse than useless to think of addictions as diseases. Second, addiction is a term that can be justly applied to many kinds of compulsive behavior besides drug-taking—for example, to gambling and compulsive eating. In line with this, there is really not much that is distinctive about psychoactive substances like heroin and alcohol in their ability to assume a controlling role in someone's life. The problem is not so much the *drugs* that people ingest, this view holds; some substances are more attractive to people than others, but no substance is inherently addictive. The real problem is that, influenced by their environment, some people come to "relate to the world through dependencies," as the addiction theorist Stanton Peele phrases it.

My feeling is that there is a great deal of insight in this position, but that it oversteps. The argument I'll be making here is that it's true there is no dark domain known as addiction whose only portal is drug abuse, but that if there is a spectrum of compulsive behavior, then certain drug addictions seem to be the most widespread and enduring compulsions we know of. Second, some substances *are* inherently addictive—not to everyone, but predictably so to large portions of the populace. A concomitant of these things is that biology matters; drug addiction cannot be reduced to an interplay between self and environment.

To the average reader, it may not be apparent why overeating deserves to be mentioned in the same breath with cocaine addiction, and I must admit that on first blush, the very idea sounds like some sort of new-age psychobabble. To understand the meaning of this idea, though, we need first to consider the two commonly accepted notions of addiction we talked about.

First, alcoholism as a disease. Is it regarded as such? My view is that no one in the United States who has watched more than two talk shows in the last year could doubt that this is the prevailing belief. For quantitative proof, though, consider that some 80 percent of the Americans who were queried in a Gallup Poll in August 1982 said they believe it is a disease.[1] As Alcoholics Anonymous has it: "Alcoholism is a disease which manifests itself chiefly by the uncontrollable drinking of the victim, who is known as an alcoholic."[2]

Well then, what kind of disease is it? That is, how is it properly categorized as such? To take one example of a more conventional disease, diabetes mellitus has a cause (a lack of insulin production) and an effect (not enough glucose getting into cells, which leads to weight loss, dehydration, and so on). To use this model in connection with alcohol, we might ask: *Where* is the disease? While science has found some intriguing physical differences between some alcoholics and nonalcoholics, nothing yet has been uncovered that would lead us to believe that alcoholics physically differ from the rest of the population in two crucial categories: alcohol craving and loss of control in connection with drinking. That such differences exist has been *assumed* to be a fact because a small minority of drinkers drink pathologically. Adding to this has been some convincing evidence that genetics can influence alcoholism.

To say that we haven't found a physical cause of alcoholism is not to say that one doesn't exist, of course, but the whole notion falls apart if alcoholics aren't, in fact, afflicted with the supposed result of their disease, a lack of control over their drinking. The University of California philosophy professor Herbert Fingarette has recently produced a book summarizing the evidence that alcoholics do not differ from the average drinker in this respect.

Loss of control? In *Heavy Drinking* Fingarette quotes longtime alcohol researcher Mark Keller on the "one drink away from a drunk" hypothesis:

What is fascinating about that slogan is that nearly all the alcoholics I have known, including those who in all sincerity proclaim that slogan, have told me that, even during the course of the severest stage of their active alcoholism, they had a drink or two or three on many occasions and stopped without further drinking, until on some other occasion, days or weeks later, they did not stop. Some could take a drink or two daily for days or weeks without going off on a bout.[3]

Fingarette cites a number of studies showing that alcoholics can, in fact, control their drinking when it suits their interest to do so. (They will refrain even in instances when they have been "primed" with doses of alcohol.)

Neither is the evidence more convincing, Fingarette says, that alcoholics have an irresistible craving for alcohol between benders:

Even if some drinkers report having felt a craving for alcohol during withdrawal, the clinical observations show that chronic drinkers often resist this craving and abstain or drink in moderation even as they are feeling withdrawal distress.[4]

Fingarette calls into question the entire classic concept of "alcoholism" to the extent that he eschews the word altogether in favor of what he believes is a more realistic term for alcohol abuse: heavy drinking. It's not necessary to accept all his ideas to admire the job he has done in deflating the highly questionable notion that alcoholism is a disease.

More to the point, for our purposes, is the common conception of opiate addiction. Here we don't need to invoke a disease concept; the overwhelming power of these drugs, this idea goes, will be enough to addict anyone who comes into frequent contact with them. A good metaphor for this is the Bela Lugosi *Dracula* movies from the 1930s. Remember Dracula's servant, Renfield? Before running into Dracula he is something of a harmless twit; once bitten, though, he must slavishly carry out Dracula's bidding. ("Master! Master!") He does not seem to do this *willingly*, but he does do it, because the fangs have dug so deep. Part of the fear generated by these movies—and by our ideas of heroin—is the notion that *any* of us could be bitten, after which our life as an autonomous being is over.

The problem with this idea in connection with hard-drug use is that it doesn't square with reality. Lots of research shows *how* wrong it is, but two strands are compelling enough that they should be convincing.

First, as to the once-bitten, always-a-slave hypothesis, we constantly have whole populations of people who are given addictive drugs in large doses over a substantial period of time, but these people subsequently evince no continuing interest in these drugs. They are hospital patients, and over time, as study after study has made clear, they show not an increasing appetite for drugs but rather an indifference to them. To take but one example, Jane Porter and Hershel Jick of Boston University Medical Center followed up on 11,882 patients who had been given narcotics to relieve pain that resulted from health problems. Of this group, only *four* went on to abuse drugs, and in only one of these cases was the abuse considered major.[5]

Things are not necessarily so much different on the street. One of the three or four most famous research projects ever carried out in connection with heroin was conducted by Lee Robins and her colleagues at Washington University in the 1970s. Robins interviewed military veterans who were returning from Vietnam in 1971. Only 2 percent of this group had tried heroin before military service, but about one-third of them used heroin in Vietnam; most of the servicemen who used narcotics did so repeatedly over a long period of time. When those who had not just used, but had become *addicted* to, narcotics returned to the United States, however, only half used heroin at all, and only 14 percent became readdicted. The lessons of this seem obvious: first, there is nothing inevitable about heroin addiction continuing once it has begun; second, the setting these veterans found themselves in had a great effect on their behavior; and third, it is quite possible to use heroin occasionally without becoming addicted to it.[6]

On this last point, consider the findings of researchers working for the Drug Abuse Council of Washington, D.C., who in 1972 interviewed 54 narcotics "chippers" of from 2 to 23 years' duration. None was involved in criminal activities (other than drug use); all were regular workers or students, and all were actively involved in social groups that had no connection with drugs. One of these people was a 33-year-old mental health worker who took cough syrup and the dependence-producing hypnotic Doriden on weekends with his wife and friends. The researchers describe his group's use thusly:

> Mr. E's weekend highs are all virtually the same. After dinner on Friday evening, he and his wife and the three couples who share their ritual congregate. They go to their respective pharmacies, get their drug, reassemble at someone's house and take their drugs. While getting "off" they decide whether to bowl, go to the movies, or sit around and listen to music. The routine is so precise that when asked why one person did not get the drugs for all of them, Mr. E simply said, "We don't do it that way."[7]

Where is the squalid crash pad in all this, the shattered lives, the tormented souls? (They are out bowling.) The message here, of course, is that addictive drug use follows no ineluctable course. It varies greatly according to the individuals involved in it.

To accept these findings is to agree that heavy drinking or addictive drug use are phenomena that can come under a great deal of human control. Writers like Herbert Fingarette and Stanton Peele are after bigger game, however, than merely knocking down rigid, flawed theories of drug and alcohol addiction. For Fingarette, once the blue smoke has been cleared around the idea of alcoholism, there is really nothing out of the ordinary left in the concept. What is alcoholism? Fingarette:

> The broad interpretation that best fits the evidence is that heavy drinkers are people for whom drinking has become a central activity in their way of life. By "central activity" I mean any hub of activity (job, religious practice, serious hobby, family or community role) that in part defines and inspires a person's identity, values, conduct, and life choices.[8]

Just because a given central activity is dysfunctional, that is no reason to believe that it can't assume the pivotal role that more productive activities do for other people. We all do self-destructive things, partly in response to the pressures we feel, his argument goes; heavy drinking is simply a meaningful, though pathological, attempt by drinkers to deal with their lives. Faced with boredom, depression, anxiety, domestic troubles—all the difficulties that go into making up a human life—one person may habitually get busy, another may get lethargic, and another may get drunk. When this turning toward alcohol happens often enough, the person is labeled an alcoholic. By the time heavy drinkers are in this condition, Fingarette says, they have come to organize their lives around the central activity of drinking; they shun abstainers and seek out opportunities to drink. They see the world in terms of its ability to hinder or facilitate their drinking. People come to this condition by way of an innumerable number of different forces, but because these forces lead to one behavior—excessive drinking—alcoholism has been assumed to have one cause, like smallpox, and is thus labeled a disease.

Stanton Peele would second most of Fingarette's notions about the bankruptcy of the disease theory of alcoholism, and he is in broad agreement with the view of hard-drug use, sketched above, that holds that it is a complex phenomenon that varies widely according to the individuals involved. Under this conception, addiction is not an all-or-nothing state like pregnancy, nor is it inevitable given exposure to drugs, nor is it permanent or even necessarily long-term.

If we thus remove the concept of drug addiction from Dracula's lair, we begin to see that it may not be so much different from other compulsive behaviors, which is precisely Peele's position. Thus:

> That addiction takes place with a range of objects, including quite common activities, drives home that no involvement or object is inherently addictive. Rather, people become addicted to a given involvement due to a combination of social and cultural, situational, personality, and developmental factors.[9]

What else could properly fall under the term addiction? Clear signs of dysfunctional compulsion have been exhibited by runners (those who repeatedly keep at it to the point of their bodies breaking down), binge eaters, and gamblers, to name a few examples.

Most of this seems perfectly sensible to me. Can anyone seriously doubt that there are pathological compulsions that have nothing to do with drugs? If, as I have argued, it is silly to think of drug addiction as a predictable and purely physical process, then what is the line that separates drug addiction from other addictions?

The school of researchers we have been talking about would say there is none at all, and I would agree that these various compulsions do not deserve to be thought of in terms of two discrete categories: drugs on one side, everything else on the other.

That said, however, it seems important to me that we reject one argument that has been forcefully stated by Peele: that no substance (or "object") is inherently addictive. Had he said that no substance is inherently addictive *to everyone,* I believe he might have had it right. But the fact is that, judging by the historical record, some substances will *inevitably* be addictive to substantial portions of the populace.

Mother nicotine is our best example here. Every society that has been touched by tobacco has taken it up with avidity. So far as I know, there have been no exceptions to this rule from the time of Columbus to the present (though some societies have been faster to accept it than others). Special groups within societies—the Mormons in the United States, for example—may successfully create nicotine-free enclaves, but they invariably do so in isolated pockets surrounded by a larger smoking society.

It's helpful to recall that the *use* of tobacco that occurs on this scale is very nearly the same thing as the *addiction* that takes place: 90 percent of all smokers, at a minimum, cannot decide to use tobacco one day and then leave it alone the next.

Alcohol is another case in point. We've noted that alcohol was abused in Roman antiquity, and, of course, it has been abused ever since. The level of its abuse has waxed and waned with different cultures and time periods, but human addiction to it has remained with us from ancient times to the present.

Cocaine and morphine are relative newcomers in this game, and the use (and abuse) of them has been far less widespread than that of nicotine and alcohol. To judge by the historical record—rather than by contemporary events—it is tempting to say that these drugs have an abuse potential far lower than that of nicotine or alcohol since, in certain places and times, they have scarcely been abused at all. (During the 1940s in the United States, cocaine was known only to a few bon vivants and hep cats.) Nevertheless, an unbroken line of addiction, however thin, does exist with these substances from the time they were first synthesized through the present.

We can get another perspective on how addictive some substances are likely to be when we look at *contemporary* society and compare drug addictions in it with other compulsions that have nothing to do with drugs.

Nicotine, as we might expect, is at the head of this parade as well. Twenty-seven percent of the adult American populace smokes, and this is one of the lower rates among Western nations.

When we turn to another drug, alcohol, the abuse figures are much smaller, but still disturbing. By one perhaps conservative estimate, somewhere between 5 and 10 percent of all adult American men could properly be called alcoholic for some part of their lives.[10] We would expect the alcoholism rate for women to be lower, by rough estimate perhaps half of the rate for men.

Having looked at these figures, our question is: How do these compulsions stack up with others that don't involve drugs?

Well, how about gambling? Estimates from England and the United States put the proportion of compulsive gamblers in those countries at something between 0.2 percent and 1 percent of the population.[11]

Anorexia nervosa? It affects perhaps 0.5 percent of the population; the figure for bulimia may be on the order of 2 percent.[12]

Scientific estimates do not seem to exist for the national prevalence of exercise addiction, but one authority on running puts the number of addicted runners in the United States at about 2.5 million people.[13] Running is, by a wide margin, the exercise that's been most studied in relation to addiction; no numbers whatever seem to exist for compulsions to perform *other* exercises. If we take a pure guess, however, and double the running figure to account for people addicted to swimming, aerobics, and so forth, we would estimate that about 2 percent of the population may be addicted to exercise.

The list of possible drugless addictions is endless, of course; if we're willing to stretch the term "addiction" into meaninglessness (television watching? excessive sleeping?) we probably could find some practices that could match the numbers put up by drug addictions. But if we look at the compulsions I've reviewed, it's apparent that all of them *together* may not affect as many people as are touched by alcoholism alone, and alcoholism, as we have seen, afflicts perhaps a quarter of the people that

tobacco addiction does. To these two chemical dependenc
then start adding the much smaller numbers for cocaine, he
the rest.

In sum, then, there are certain drugs that have shown a great attractiveness to the human race over time, through cultures and, in the contemporary world at least, in comparison with other nondrug compulsions.

What we begin to get from this is a sense that biology matters.
What is one clear difference between drug addictions and other addictions? Drugs have *direct* biological effects, whereas nondrug compulsions do not. The appeal of a drug like nicotine seems to spread across
all cultures and times; when we see this, we might infer that nicotine has
this appeal because of its effects on the one thing that all cultures have
in common: the human body.

This may seem painfully obvious until we consider the fact that
there is a school of thought that rigorously rejects all notions of
"biological determinism" in drug abuse. What matters in drug abuse
under this view? An individual's circumstances, his temperament, the
psychological wounds he bears, and the meaning he comes to give to his
addiction.

To all these assertions I say, amen; these things count. I would sum
up this reasoning in this way: if drug addiction requires a kind of
agreement between self and substance, then individuals bring at least as
much to drugs as drugs bring to individuals.

Environment and social class have an unquestioned effect on drug
abuse. In many addictions, there is a large component of defeatism, of
bad self-image, and of negative outlook. Stanton Peele notes this when
he quotes the psychologist Isidor Chein on a street heroin addict that
Chein and his colleagues followed. In paraphrase:

> Unlike others, he could not find a vocation, a career, a meaningful,
> sustained activity around which he could wrap his life. Instead, he
> relied on the addiction to provide a vocation around which he could
> build a reasonably full life and establish an identity, albeit a negative
> one.[14]

The gist of this argument in relation to drugs is that people who
become addicts don't have enough of a life *outside* of drugs to induce

them to stay away from these substances. Of course this is true. Is it any accident that heroin and crack cocaine run through the hopeless streets of America's ghettos like so much sewer water, while the folks who live up on the hill are hardly touched by this? The 11,000 hospital patients we talked about earlier—the ones who quit taking drugs once their illness was over—did so in part because they had lives that were worth getting back to.

There is another persuasive person/environment argument about drug use that has to do with what we might call the investment of self in substance. Addicts come to believe in the substance they are using, believe in its power, and this praise-song comes to influence their behavior.

We can see this phenomenon in the drinker who uses his alcohol consumption as an excuse to be loud and obnoxious, or the cocaine user who "finds" himself sexually voracious when he's snorted a few lines. People come to assign meanings to the substances they use; with these substances they become what they had a yearning to be anyway. Then the "power" the drug has over them increases in this self-invented way when they assume they can't be what they want *without* using the drug.

In motivational factors like these, we have, it seems to me, concepts that have great utility in explaining drug abuse. In agreeing that things like this are important, however, we have to be careful not to throw the baby out with the bathwater. Put simply, we need to recognize that substances themselves are important; that some are, in fact, *inherently* rewarding (or, in their absence, punishing) without reference to the investment of self or problems of environment.

How do we know? Well, animals presumably have no investment of self in cocaine, yet they'll press levers for it until they die. The smokers in the NIDA experiments we reviewed earlier did not know what drug it was they were getting intravenously, but when it was nicotine they pressed levers for it at nice, steady intervals, dosing themselves in an extremely controlled way. When, however—unbeknownst to them— saline started coming through the tubes, their lever pressing became disordered and decreased as time went on. The multiple drug abusers NIDA recruited had no idea what drugs they were being dosed with, yet the ones they liked, it turned out, were the very ones that we find people abusing out in the real world.

That some substances have an inherent abuse liability does
vitiate the importance of human choice or of individual variability
need to be clear that the attractions of drugs are in part biologica ven
this, it is next to impossible to imagine the societal conditions that would
make the attractiveness of these substances disappear altogether.

Stanton Peele is very much persuaded by the argument of personal
and social affliction as it relates to addiction and, from it, he fashions his
notion of our best hope to deal with addiction. As he has written with
Archie Brodsky:

> The best antidotes to addiction are joy and competence—joy as the
> capacity to take pleasure in the people, activities, and things that are
> available to us; competence as the ability to master relevant parts of
> the environment and the confidence that our actions make a dif-
> ference for ourselves and others.[15]

But what does tobacco use tell us about this? Well, unlike the case
with, say, heroin, it's difficult to believe that most smokers keep smoking because they see their world as limited. Most of them are mastering
their environment just fine, thanks; many of them have a great deal of
competence in a wide variety of areas, and the practice of smoking
interferes little with their ability to broaden themselves further. If a
sense of a limited life is crucial to driving people to compulsive practices, then in the 1950s, half the men in the United States would have
to have been suffering from this affliction as a precursor to taking up,
and staying with, this habit.

Peele correctly points out that many addictions are subject to a
syndrome called "maturing out": drug abusers simply quit taking drugs
when they get older. The common interpretation of this is that increasing years bring increasing responsibilities and that responsibilities make
drug users shape up. But, Peele writes, "When people fail to outgrow
addiction . . . it is because they are unable either to develop adult skills
or to become a part of normal social networks."[16]

The problem with this in relation to tobacco is that (*a*) smokers
have no problem developing adult skills or becoming a part of social
networks and (*b*) they don't mature out. The first part of this statement
speaks for itself; the second part requires some explanation.

At first glance, it's not too surprising that the maturing-out process that goes on with other drugs doesn't take place with nicotine. It's difficult, though not impossible, to be a heroin addict and live a responsible life, but it's quite common to be a smoker *and* get the lawn mowed on Saturday. Given this, there is little about adulthood that inclines smokers toward quitting.

But if we look a little closer, it seems to me that there is a lesson here. If drug abuse is critically motivated by economic, social, and personal afflictions, then why don't we see some dramatic changes in the prevalence of smoking as people go from young to old? Emotional forces are bound to change in this transition; economic exigencies will as well. Under Peele's notions, we would, if anything, expect a greater prevalence of smoking in younger years, given the abundance of emotional and economic problems during that time.

Instead, what we see with smoking is, first, a relative constancy of it over all age groups. (In 1985, 29 percent of white American men aged 18 to 24 smoked; among 55- to 64-year-olds, 30 percent smoked.)[17] Second, we see rates going *up* a little as adolescents become young adults; then rates decline slightly as middle age sets in.

What I see in this is a compulsion that is, to a large degree, immune from the forces of economic and emotional change. What I see in it is a kind of statistical counterpart to those NIDA experiments in which smokers could dose themselves with nicotine just by pushing a lever. They did exactly that at a steady pace, pushing for the drug at predictable rates over long periods of time. Regular smokers do this too in a sense, only they do it over a lifetime; dosing at 18, they're probably still dosing at 40 and 55.

Those who cannot stop may stay with this habit in part because of the limitations they feel in various aspects of their lives; they undoubtedly stay with the habit because it has become an unhealthy means of relating to their environment. But they smoke in response to these forces because the drug that smoking delivers is inherently powerful. It has a great ability to reward smokers when they take it and to punish them when they don't. If it did not have this power, users would not stay with it for long in the first place. This power is in large part biological and, as such, it does no good to act as though any economic change or alteration in societal consciousness is going to end the addictive liability of drugs like nicotine. This latter proposition has great importance when we begin to ponder the question of how, as a society, we should respond to the problem of drug abuse.

• • •

If, as I have argued, people take drugs for a variety of reasons, each of which contributes some increment of motivation to the habit, then it follows that we don't have to eliminate *all* the motivations that are present to stop a given practice; we only have to eliminate some critical proportion of them. If it is true, as I've argued, that biology matters, then it follows that we should place some priority on biology—with research on receptors and nerve pathways and neurotransmitters—as a means of ascertaining whether drug debilitation can be lessened through a sufficient understanding of drug effects at the biological level. I believe, in fact, that the priority we place on biological work ought to be very high for the simple reason that it is the only approach that holds out the chance of anything like victory in this struggle, although the chances of even it succeeding seem slim.

The really relevant question, though, is: What else do we have? There is one other approach that stands to keep us in place at best, another that stands to be beneficial, though not spectacularly so. And then there is biology: terra incognita on our map but, like any unexplored territory, of potentially great value.

What won't work? Suppressive state power aimed at punishing users and eliminating the supply of drugs. Nations have had vast experience with this, but by my rough count, in our century this has worked precisely once: with opium in China through the tender mercies of the communists after 1949. (The penalty there for relapsing after drug rehabilitation was execution.) The history of tobacco is rife with attempts, always futile, to forcibly eliminate use of the bitter weed. The prohibition of alcohol in the United States early in this century is perhaps the greatest modern example of suppressionist folly.

This is not to say that state power has no effect: Americans clearly did consume less alcohol during Prohibition, and we have reason to believe that the massive state power employed against drugs in the

United States now acts in the manner of a very leaky roof: things are bad with it but they would be much worse without it.

The fact is, however, that drug abuse waxes and wanes in societies with little regard for whatever suppressive measures governments take. State power as it affects drug supply is, at best, a holding action that is monstrously wasteful in terms of lives and resources. It amounts to an attempt to douse burning buildings when we need instead to attend to the causes of our fires.

Better prospects for success exist with efforts to diminish demand for drugs. Cigarette smoking is an excellent example of this. In the United States, beginning in the mid-1960s, a band of health advocacy groups, government officials, and individual mavericks had the courage to begin taking on the multibillion-dollar tobacco industry and its friends in Congress in an effort to get Americans to quit smoking. Their success has been astonishing by standard of comparison with other nations, and they have accomplished this feat mostly by supplying information to the public.

Over the years, these people primarily have been making a health case in connection with smoking, but they have, of course, been fighting a *drug* battle to a large degree. The good news here is that education can work. The bad news is that its power seems to be limited and slow-acting; while 40 percent of the adult American populace smoked in 1964, 27 percent of the populace is smoking now. The change has been huge in absolute numbers, but it leaves a lot to be desired. Education syndromes analogous to this take place in connection with many other drugs of abuse.

We know something, then, about police power and demand reduction in relation to what they are likely to do to palliate our drug problem. What is largely unknown, however, is what neuroscience might be able to do for us.

I admit at the outset that this is another way of saying that biological research is a pig in a poke. Further, I admit that there good reasons to be cynical about whether this approach *could* work.

Our primary reason to be optimistic is that real advances have been made in the neurobiology of drug use in the past 20 years, in general terms with the description of specific substance receptors and the pinpointing of neural pathways for drugs. Another encouraging sign is the appearance of testable theories of the biology of drug abuse, as with the medial forebrain bundle hypothesis. (This theory is particularly hopeful, it's worth noting, because it posits a single mechanism that is involved in most of our serious drug problems.)

Beyond this, neurobiology already has something of a track record: two notable advances in demand reduction for drugs have come from pharmacology in the form of nicotine gum and methadone. These substances are admittedly ineffective in many instances, perhaps even counterproductive in some ways. But we are much better off with them than without them.

Running against this good news is the state of our knowledge regarding the biology of drug abuse. God is truly in the details in neurobiology, and scientists working in this field are up against a bewildering complexity. We are nowhere near understanding drug effects at the ground-floor level of biology; reaching this point may take so long that it makes a hash out of the idea that this is an "approach" to dealing with drugs.

Moreover, one could take the view that this task is theoretically hopeless, since what is being sought is a means, probably pharmacological, to make people decline to do what they manifestly want to do so very much: get high. The desire for a magic bullet is ever present in human affairs, but in this case the search is foolish, this view holds, because what we are fighting is not an impersonal enemy, like the polio virus, but human desire itself.

Furthermore, there is the view that whatever advances science makes in this area simply will be used by the other side—by illegal drug designers and other entrepreneurs of addiction. This certainly has been true in the past: heroin was first produced on a large scale and marketed at the turn of the century by the Bayer Company (yes, the aspirin company), which was acting in part on the sincere, yet mistaken, belief that the new drug could help cure morphine addiction. Under this view, scientific research on this subject amounts to a kind of self-defeating pharmacological arms race.

Finally, this issue raises questions about social control. It is one thing to imagine developing drug *substitutes* like methadone and nicotine gum. It is quite another, however, to imagine developing processes or substances that are aimed at altering human desire. Do we really want this latter capability, no matter what its benefits may be?

All of these are serious challenges, but it is by no means clear that it's impossible to surmount them. (Why can't we have a substance that leaves people functional, unharmed, and satisfied?) Even with these difficulties, I believe we should strive to attain a deep understanding of the biology of addiction because it may yield the benefits we've talked about. In practical terms, I am making a case here for a strategic decision that the brain is a primary battlefield in the war on drugs. An understanding of this, it seems to me, would allow society to begin channeling money more appropriately in this fight. (It's clear we don't do this now: in the current year, 70 percent of all congressional drug abuse funding will go toward supply suppression.)[18] An added advantage of this approach is that work on the neurobiology of drug abuse has great spin-off potential for many areas of human disease—Parkinson's and Alzheimer's come to mind—just as work on AIDS is invaluable in our coming to a general understanding of the body's immune system.

Beyond these practical motivations, however, I believe we should work toward obtaining this knowledge for reasons having to do with human potential and aspiration.

Addiction is a notion at once fearful and exotic because it sits apart from so much of our experience. We may choose to smoke a cigarette or to read a book, but only the cigarette can *demand* our attention. Addiction has to do with power, with the ceding of the will, with the loss an autonomous self. Because this drama can be played out elsewhere—in romantic relationships, for example—it's not surprising that we turn to addiction repeatedly as a *concept* in describing phenomena that have nothing to do with chemical substances. Yet it is to drugs that we invariably return to define our notion of addiction, with other compulsions being judged "addictive" in accordance with how much they are like drug dependence.

Unfortunately, in our society, confessions to still lesser "addictions"—to chocolate or opera—usually are announced with as much pride as embarrassment; with a sense that to be driven to do something is only human. Thus do we get the cachet of addiction in modern America, which lends a patina of attraction to real addiction, especially to those, like young people, who are overly impressed by image. Too late do some of them learn that real addiction is not an indulgence, like too much lipstick, but a wretched condition.

Only human? At its extremes, drug dependence often is not only the loss of an autonomous self; it is the loss of a self altogether. There is a saying among addicts that deep into addiction, all junkies become the same person. There is but one need; there is but one set of activities to be carried out; there is but one reaction to fulfilling the need. Personality, intellect, differing interests—all the things that make us human eventually are swallowed up into the maw of the solitary pursuit.

Things are different with nicotine in this regard only because it is legal, it produces less tolerance, and its immediate effects are less debilitating; even with these differences we can still see this phenomenon around the edges of tobacco use. Consider the fact that for centuries approximately one-third of the population has daily and repeatedly offended *itself* and the other two-thirds of the populace by fouling the air and spitting black juice onto whatever space has been handy. Tobacco users have run roughshod over their own sense of human decorum and become these spitting, spewing automata because their need is that strong.

Looked at one way, drug abuse has come about because, as a species, we humans have been half-clever. Clever enough to realize more than a thousand years ago that opium could quell the pain of disease; not clever enough to control the savior that we had found. Clever enough to calm ourselves with nicotine; not clever enough to realize that the relaxation came at a price. Clever enough to distill morphine and cocaine from the plants that nature provided; not clever enough to use their wondrous potency strictly for good.

Now, however, we have a chance to be fully clever. We have a chance to ensure that all the things we regard as most human—free will, individuality, morality—are not smothered by the incoherent impulses seated deep in our crania. As it happens, most of the drugs of abuse we have talked about have their most potent biological effects there, in the primitive parts of our brains developed by our reptilian ancestors. The work going on to challenge the effects of these drugs, though, is being carried out in our species' true crown, the higher brain we call the cerebral cortex. This is a race we should run to prove who we are.

Advice on Quitting

THIS HAS BEEN very much a book of ideas about smoking, which is another way of saying that there hasn't been much offered here in the way of practical information. While it's odd to change horses so far across stream, it seemed to me almost laughably academic to produce a work that goes into such rich detail on why people smoke without saying anything about what may be the most crucial issue in smoking: how to stop doing it. (As a man I once knew in Kansas would have said, a person who could produce a book on smoking without this information would have to be "all beard and no head.")

Hence, I set forth here the most up-to-date knowledge about quitting I have been able to gather from the scientific research that's been conducted on the subject.[1]

Giving advice about how to quit smoking, I should note, amounts to an exercise in letting people in on probabilities: no one can say for sure what stop-smoking techniques will work for any given person. Since no two people *stay* with this complex habit for exactly the same reasons, it's not surprising that no two people are likely to *leave* the act in exactly the same way. All science can do is provide a basis for making bets: if you do this, you are more likely to be able to quit than if you do that.

Scientific research yielded up the news, years ago, that no single stop-smoking technique—behavioral deconditioning or anti-nicotine drugs or whatever—could be expected to knock out the habit all by itself. Nor, it turns out, is any single technique likely to be as effective as a whole set of techniques used in combination.

But which set? There's the rub. No front-runner has yet emerged, and it seems unlikely that any will, because of the highly individualistic match between self and smoking we talked about. Given this, what I have done is to select from the literature a number of techniques that seem to me to work well together. I don't cover the waterfront here; there are many well-reasoned approaches that I don't mention. I have left them out simply because I didn't want to create a numbing laundry list of ideas. Overburdening the reader with advice may, in fact, be a problem with the list I *have* presented. For the smoker who is trying to give up the habit, quitting may seem like an act of such heroism that nothing further should be required; what I've presented here may simply seem like too much to ask.

Therefore, keep in mind that it's not necessary to employ *everything* I suggest in every attempt to quit. Feel free to pick and choose. Indeed, a first principle in my advice is that the journey to freedom belongs to the smoker; it is his or hers to construct in a profound sense. This is so because smoking is *not* a disease or a condition, but rather is a human behavior. As such, it can be brought under human control. And the elements that go into quitting are always the same: one human, one addiction, one act of pluck and intelligence, generally long-term.

The first advice I would give to anyone trying to quit is: You can do this. Millions of people have, and they were no more "hooked" than you are, nor were they more clever or resolute than you are. You stand to do yourself a lot of good if you keep this in mind. What millions of others can do, *you* can do as well. Why should it be otherwise? Don't do yourself the disservice of imagining that you are special in some negative sense. I would encourage you not to pass lightly over this point as if the "real" advice were yet to come, but to consider it and take it to heart: internalize it, as the modern slogan has it, because it matters. You have the power to do this.

The next thing I would say is that you should not regard any attempt at quitting as some all-or-nothing battle whose outcome will seal your fate. The odds are high—very high—that it will take anyone several tries to quit smoking. This is so for the simple reason that, for most people, it's damn difficult to stop. But stopping smoking is no different from any other difficult thing in that it can be more readily mastered *with learning and practice*. And *this* is how you should regard any attempt at quitting: as an exercise in learning. After an honest attempt to quit, a relapse to smoking is no more a "failure" than hitting a golf ball into a tree would be during one's first outing.

In fact, this whole process can be likened to . . . developing a *good golf game*. What do you need for this? Well, you need to develop a drive off the tee, a good approach shot to the green, and putting ability. You also need to learn how to avoid traps like the ponds and the roughs, and you need to avoid those trees we talked about.

It's no different with stopping smoking. You need to learn what works and—just as important—you need to learn what doesn't work; you need to learn what is going to land you in a difficult situation in which you'll be likely to smoke.

Any attempt to stop smoking may be the one that will allow you to quit forever, and every attempt should be undertaken with the idea that permanent abstinence is an entirely achievable outcome. If you fail to reach this goal, however, keep in mind that you have *lots* of company; there is nothing "wrong" with you because you did not succeed in a given attempt. You should take what you can from your effort, which may be a great deal. When were you tempted to smoke? Why were you tempted to smoke? What can you learn about this for the next effort? (Which should be coming up soon.) To judge by the experience of hundreds of others, it is worse than useless for smokers who "slip" to berate themselves for this fact. Most smokers who finally quit spend some time moving in and out of smoking first. This may well be your experience; learn from it.

A question for anyone who is considering quitting is: Do I do this by myself, or do I seek help? For what guidance it provides, 85 to 95 percent of all smokers who quit do so on their own. It would be reasonable for first-time quitters to assume they are similar to people in this large majority and therefore to try to pull off the trick without help. On the other hand, measured 12 months out, stay-quit rates are a little worse for people who make one attempt at quitting by themselves compared to people who seek professional help. Since we're making bets here, the advice I would give is this: if it's one of your initial attempts at quitting, try it by yourself. If you've tried to quit repeatedly, however, only to go back to smoking, then you probably should think about entering a program.

If a program is for you, the question is, which one? Three national nonprofit organizations run well-respected programs in many communities across the country. They are the American Cancer Society, the American Lung Association, and the Seventh Day Adventist Church. To find out if these organizations are sponsoring stop-smoking programs in your area, simply call up their local affiliate or church.

If you decide to do this on your own, there's some advance work to take care of before you actually quit. A question you might want to ask yourself is: How *much* do I want to do this? If the answer is that it's occurred to you or you wouldn't mind stopping, then you might want to reconsider and wait until you have a stronger desire to quit. Motivation can be important, and you may be doing yourself a disservice by going into this half-heartedly. If your desire to quit is low and doesn't change much over long periods of time, then you should probably go ahead and make an attempt, since one period of time is likely to be the same as the next in terms of your desire. If your motivation waxes and wanes a fair amount, however, then you might want to wait until you have some fire in your belly before going forward.

You might also want to ask yourself: *Why* do I want to quit? A fuzzy, generalized notion that smoking is bad for your health won't do here. Get out a piece of paper and write down the reasons you'd like to quit. Will it ease things up for you at work? Will it make you more attractive? What about the cost? Are you worried about the effect on your children? Think about all these things and write them down; know why you're going into this.

Regard this as a contest, a struggle; you have an enemy, which is smoking. As in any contest, it is helpful to know as much as possible about the opposition before entering into the fray. What do you know about your own smoking habit? When do you smoke your first cigarette of the day? Which cigarettes of the day do you really crave, which are simply pleasurable, and which are you relatively indifferent to? Where do you smoke cigarettes? Get to know your own smoking habit; it would probably be helpful to construct a record of the cigarettes you smoke during the day, noting when and where they were smoked and rating each of them as to their desirability. What's the contour of your habit? When does it rise and fall? Knowing more about it can only do you good.

What else should your planning include? Well, think about what's coming up in your life and how it will interact with quitting. Since one of the things that's likely to be a problem is weight gain (about which more in a minute), it stands to reason that it might not be a good idea to quit right around Christmas. Stress will probably be a *big* enemy, so you may not want to try to stop in the weeks before a major project will be due at work.

Next, you probably could benefit from employing a strategy known as "nicotine fading," which simply means reducing your nicotine intake by switching brands several times over a period of, say, three weeks, each time going to a brand with a lower tar and nicotine rating; all this leads up to the day on which you'll quit altogether.

Now, as we have seen, smokers can easily undercut the effect of low-tar and nicotine cigarettes by covering up the perforation holes around their filters, by taking bigger, deeper drags, by smoking the cigarette farther down, and so forth. Even with the best intentions, it is likely you'll be doing some of this compensating. Nevertheless, you should be able to reduce your nicotine intake over time by buying cigarettes with lower tar and nicotine ratings.

How can you calculate a fading rate? Use a percentage system. Look at the tar and nicotine ratings of your current cigarette. Then, in your first week of fading, buy a brand that's lower by 30 percent; in the second week, go to 60 percent; and in the third week, cut down by 90 percent. (All this assumes you are not currently smoking "ultra-light" cigarettes, which don't leave you much room to fade.) Doing this will not only ease you into abstinence, but will make you much more conscious of smoking (of when you most want cigarettes, and so forth), which should be helpful.

There is another technique that can make you conscious of a particular feature of smoking: how filthy it is. Do this in the two weeks before you quit: throw all your butts in a clear glass jar and after a week or so, fill the thing half up with water; continue throwing butts in until the day you quit and keep the jar in a visually prominent place even after you stop. Its charming appearance should be an inspiration to you as you move into abstinence.

Next, go to your doctor and get a prescription for nicotine gum. As I write this, a debate is running through the research community about the effectiveness of this product, but two of its benefits seem clear: it should cut down on the withdrawal symptoms you will feel, and it should at least delay the increase in weight you are likely to experience. (The gum should be particularly helpful in reducing weight gain if you tended to smoke while active.) These are not inconsiderable effects; a large proportion of smokers cannot make it past the first few days of withdrawal, and nicotine gum will help. It is the combination of abstinence effects that can whipsaw many people back into smoking very quickly after they try to quit. You're likely to have enough problems quitting *with* nicotine gum; you don't need to try this without it.

Your doctor will have to advise you on how to use nicotine gum— on how many pieces to use at what intervals, and so forth. Do not accept a 15-second lecture over the phone on this; see your doctor face to face or have him phone you when he has some time to explain to you as much as he can about how to use it. The more advice you get, the more effective the gum is likely to be for you.

Here are a few things I should tell you about the gum in case your doctor leaves them out. First, when you get it, use it regularly. This advice is not as ridiculous as it sounds; many people seem to get the gum and then not chew it. Second, the nicotine in the gum enters your bloodstream through your mouth lining, not through your stomach. It does no good to be swallowing the juices produced by the gum. Third, consuming just about anything but tap water before chewing the gum will render it relatively ineffective. (Coffee or carbonated drinks or fruit juices create a pH environment in the mouth that keeps the nicotine from being absorbed.) Wait about 15 minutes after eating or drinking anything before beginning to chew the gum, and then, of course, don't drink *while* chewing.

In your preparation phase, set a definite day to quit and then don't monkey with it. The day you are going to quit will mean something; you should act accordingly. You may wish to go public with your intention of quitting as a means of ensuring a serious effort beginning on day one: tell some friends or co-workers of what you intend to do and when you intend to do it.

Finally, you may wish not only to notify, but to enlist the support of, some of these people. When you tell a spouse, partner, or co-worker of your intention to quit, let them know that you're likely to be irritable, distracted, perhaps depressed on and off for a period of time, and that you'd appreciate their understanding. Research has made clear that this kind of support can be helpful in succeeding; why not enlist it?

Those who are put off by the idea of asking for support may have a higher level lesson to learn here: being smart will get you a lot further in this effort than being strong. While willpower is valuable, it is perhaps the *least* important weapon in any stop-smoking arsenal. In the job you have to do, willpower alone will not cut it, and willpower in tandem with other things will go only so far. Think of it in terms of hauling a load of bricks with a wheelbarrow. You could try to *carry* the thing, but you'll probably get farther by rolling it along the ground. Your goal is to stop smoking, not to prove how strong you are.

This notion will serve you in good stead when you reach the day you're actually going to quit. What kind of day should that be? Here's a suggestion: make it a weekend day in which you can stay reasonably busy outside the house doing enjoyable things. This advice follows from several principles that you might want to draw on throughout your effort.

First, recall from Chapter 5 that while users of some drugs may want to get *high,* smokers seem to want to get *medium* from their drug of choice. If you think about it, it follows from this that anything that pulls you much off-center may prompt the urge to smoke in you. To take the extremes, hammering tension at work will pull you one way, but a wildly exuberant time at a rock club will pull you another. In either event, your response might well be: I need a cigarette. For a fair amount of time after you've quit smoking, what you want to do is avoid emotional extremes in either direction to the extent you can. In general, the safest state for you is one of mild relaxation and stimulation.

Principle two has to do with what we looked at in Chapter 10 on behavioral conditioning. Recall that people come to associate their smoking very closely with certain acts or objects. Do you always smoke while doing the crossword puzzle? It's not a bad bet that starting to work on a puzzle now will prompt an urge to smoke. Likewise for lying on your favorite couch and watching football, if you were used to smoking in that situation. Ditto for driving to work.

This is obviously a hell of a problem, since you either *like* to do these things or you *need* to do them. How should you handle this? Well, try altering these things just a little. Sit in another chair while watching football. Work the crossword out on the front steps. Take the bus to work.

As you can see, what you'll be doing here is making a path for yourself through your life—a path that is not strewn with this disease-producing means of relating to everything in your environment. Nicotine was a very *attractive* means of relating to these things; it did something for you. But that's over. Now it's you and the activities and objects in your life without the middleman.

As a practical matter, urges to smoke can be set off not only by *activities* that have been paired with smoking, but by any smoking-related "cue." The sight of an ashtray will do it; a pack of matches, even. So? Get rid of all the things in your home and workplace that are directly associated with smoking. Throw away your cigarettes, of course, but also give away your lighter and dump your ashtrays.

It's tempting to say that people who have spouses or partners who smoke might want to get rid of them too, but it turns out that the evidence is a little weak on this. It's not clear whether having a smoking partner will significantly hurt your chances for success. The best advice if you're in this situation is to come to an understanding in advance with your partner that he or she will not smoke in your presence.

The advice on what to do about friends who smoke is more straightforward: try to avoid them for awhile. At a minimum, make sure they don't smoke when you're around. People who have friends who smoke are clearly at a greater risk of relapsing.

This is not surprising, since in perhaps *half* of all relapse episodes, the ex-smoker gets his cigarettes from another smoker. (Not because a cigarette been forced on him, however; he usually asks for one.) Up to three-quarters of all relapse episodes occur in situations in which someone is smoking near the ex-smoker. The message of this is clear: stay away from smoky environments. (Bars are excellent places to avoid because they have not only smoke in them, but alcohol as well, which weakens resistance to temptation.)

You should be aware that you'll probably experience abstinence in two fairly distinct phases: withdrawal, which should last at most two weeks, and then "protracted abstinence," which, while probably less severe, is in some ways more dangerous. In withdrawal, you're likely to have some of the symptoms we talked about in Chapter 7: sleeplessness, an inability to concentrate, anxiety, and so forth. These things may be more or less constant in you for awhile, and it is in connection with them that nicotine gum stands to do you a lot of good.

Within a few days, though, you'll probably notice these withdrawal symptoms easing up. After awhile your urges to smoke may be widely separated in time; your withdrawal may lighten enough that you can go for long stretches without the desire to smoke hanging over you like some low-grade fever. The message to take from this, however, is not that you've won, but rather that phase two has begun.

Once it's under way, what many people report is that, in a moment in which they were feeling no withdrawal symptoms whatsoever, they suddenly wanted a cigarette, had access to one, and—bang—found themselves smoking again. In other cases, a more familiar sounding relapse syndrome occurs: a smoker will have a craving and give into it.

Regarding this latter sort of relapse, here's a piece of information you might find useful. Smokers often seem to believe that these cravings go on forever. Actually, they tend to last three to five minutes. Think of that when a craving comes up: three to five minutes and you're on your way out of it. You can make it past almost anything for this amount of time, and craving a cigarette should be no exception.

Regarding relapsing in general, there are two main lines of defense. The first, which we've already talked a little about, is to avoid high-risk situations. The second, which is more important, is to develop what are known in the trade as "coping mechanisms."

A smoking researcher named Saul Shiffman has been a great source of knowledge on both of these things. For several years, Shiffman and his colleagues ran a telephone service called the Stay-Quit Line, which was set up to aid ex-smokers who were experiencing relapse crises. In counseling the people who called, Shiffman's staff were able to find out a lot about the conditions under which smokers are tempted to relapse and what *responses* are effective in keeping this from occurring.

We've already reviewed some of the general conditions that are likely to lead to relapse: extreme psychological states, being around other smokers, and so forth. Shiffman and his co-workers, however, have been able to put a finer point on some of these things. What conditions lead to relapse?

Stress, for one. Half the Stay-Quit callers reported having substantial levels of stress in the hours before their crises, and stress was a very potent force in actually making them light up, as opposed to just thinking about it.

Stress is just one feeling, however, in a whole constellation of negative emotions that helps prompt relapse. Anger, frustration, and depression are others. Three-quarters of the people who called Stay-Quit reported some kind of negative emotion as an immediate antecedent of their crisis. The state of feeling bad is very dangerous territory for the ex-smoker.

These emotions are likely to be particularly tricky in two situations: being home alone—while not doing much of anything—and being at work, particularly while under performance pressure. Anxiety and frustration are states that frequently lead to crises in both environments, while the home-alone situation also has depression associated with it.

Positive moods, however, can be dangerous as well. More than half the Stay-Quit callers had a relapse crisis on the heels of eating or drinking; almost 20 percent had drunk alcohol and almost 20 percent had drunk coffee. Many of these situations occur in the home, obviously, but an evening out can present a particularly wicked combination of factors: food, friends who smoke, and alcohol. When the ex-smoker is feeling good, these smoking cues seem to be particularly important.

When we look at all these situations—positive and negative—it is obvious that most of them cannot be avoided. (Working? Eating?) So what can a person do?

The thing to do is to learn to *cope*. Shiffman has found that 70 percent of ex-smokers who produce a coping response in a crisis do not relapse in that situation, while only 18 percent of those who do not generate a response manage to stay abstinent.

What's a coping response? Shiffman divides them into two types: cognitive and behavioral, which we might think of simply as *thinking* on the one hand, and *doing* on the other. What are some thinking mechanisms that work? Think about how much it will benefit your health not to smoke, or how much it will hurt your health *to* smoke. Distract yourself by thinking about something else altogether. Go over your reasons for quitting.

And behavioral mechanisms? Well, there's always *flight* from the situation. Get up from the dining room table; leave the meeting for a while. (Remember, it's better to be smart here than to be strong.) How about carrying some low-calorie candy around with you to suck on? Distract yourself by doing something else. Play video games, go cook something. Get your body moving with some energetic physical exercise.

Regarding this last suggestion, it's worth noting how many pins this one activity will knock down. When you quit smoking, you're likely to have problems with (among other things) stress, weight gain, sleeplessness, work, and moments of cigarette craving. Regular aerobic physical exercise (such as brisk walking or swimming) can help with every one of these things. It cuts down on weight gain, and we have good reason to believe it elevates work performance, reduces sleeplessness, and improves mood—not just for an hour or two, mind you, but *generally*. Furthermore, exercise is obviously a good coping mechanism, since it is very difficult to light a cigarette while jogging.

Even so, exercise obviously has limited value as a coping mechanism since you can't do it very often or in very many environments. So you might want to develop some behavioral coping skills that can be undertaken nearly everywhere, at any time, and that can have the generalized effect of reducing stress. I'm thinking here of deep, slow breathing with eyes closed—probably the best thing for an immediate crisis—and of meditation. Neither is difficult to do, and either can be employed while sitting in an office chair.

One important thing to recognize about abstinence and coping is that, while relapse crises are likely to get less and less frequent the longer a smoker has stayed quit, coping mechanisms also seem to be used less frequently the further out smokers get. The thing to do is to stay vigilant; you might want to write down some of your coping mechanisms on a piece of paper to carry in your wallet or purse. That way you won't be caught off guard if something happens a good distance downstream.

Recall that I began this discussion by urging smokers to regard any *failed* attempt at quitting as an opportunity for learning. With what we've just reviewed, it may be apparent that, in your learning exercise, the two most important questions you want to answer are: When was I tempted to smoke? and what coping mechanisms kept me from giving in? The more systematic you are about collecting this information, the better off you'll be.

Finally, there is no reason that the ex-smoker who has one cigarette needs to go on to have any more. Smoking one cigarette is just that; it is not going to kindle some uncontrollable urge in you for more. Don't kid yourself about this as a backdoor way to resume smoking for awhile. Cut your losses and go on.

Many of the things I've suggested here—not going to bars, taking up jogging, doing meditation, and so forth—may seem about as attractive as a cold shower. But think for a moment about what it is you're actually doing when you quit smoking. You are leaving something that provided you with a number of things you liked: calmness, alertness, and a reduced waistline possibly among them. Unfortunately, smoking also provided you with addiction, expense, odor, and the good possibility of an early grave.

What's important to recognize is that you're still going to want the calmness and alertness and so forth after you've quit; the trick is to get these things through life-enhancing practices rather than a life-suffocating one. Things like exercise and meditation should not be thought of as busywork you've taken up to keep from smoking, but as part of a transformation of self—a transformation in which you will increasingly relate to your world through healthy, rather than pathological, means.

If you're like most people, the further out you get from quitting, the less frequent your cravings will become and the less often it will even occur to you to have a cigarette. Smoking will become a smaller and smaller object in your internal landscape, as if it were a city skyline you were watching diminish while departing on a ship.

Your work will be finished when you find yourself one day in a situation that you once knew as particularly dangerous for relapse. It may hit you, some time into this, that you haven't even *thought* about having a cigarette and can't imagine lighting up. At that moment, you'll be able to take justifiable pleasure and pride in the fact that you call the shots now; the captain of your ship is you.

References

CHAPTER 1
Why Do People Do That?

1. Bartolome De Las Casas, in Sarah A. Dickson, *Panacea or Precious Bane: Tobacco in Sixteenth-Century Literature* (New York: New York Public Library, 1954), p. 106.

2. Horace Greeley, in Jerome E. Brooks, *The Mighty Leaf: Tobacco through the Centuries* (Boston: Little, Brown, 1952), p. 219.

3. Bob Newhart, "Introducing Tobacco to Civilization," from *The Button-Down Mind on TV* (Warner Brothers Records, 1962).

4. J. Richard Eiser et al., "Smokers, Non-smokers and the Attribution of Addiction." *British Journal of Social Clinical Psychology* 16 (1977): 329–36.

5. Ibid.

6. M. A. H. Russell, "The Smoking Habit and Its Classification." *The Practitioner* 212 (1974), p. 794.

7. Jerome Jaffe, "Keynote Remarks." In *The Pharmacologic Treatment of Tobacco Dependence* (Cambridge: The Institute for the Study of Smoking Behavior and Policy, Harvard University, 1986), p. 7.

8. Russell, "The Smoking Habit," p. 793.

9. Saul Shiffman, "A Cluster-Analytic Classification of Smoking Relapse Episodes." *Addictive Behaviors* 11 (1986): 295–307.

10. Ibid.

11. Jack Henningfield, interview with the author (August 18, 1987).

CHAPTER 2
Outside the Chemical Realm

1. W. A. Hunt and J. D. Matarazzo, "Habit Mechanisms in Smoking." In *Learning Mechanisms in Smoking,* ed. W. A. Hunt (Chicago: Aldine Publishing Co., 1970), p. 74.

2. James Boswell, *Journal of the Tour to the Hebrides* (London, 1785). Quoted in the Arents Collection Catalogue, vol. 4, no. 941 (New York Public Library), p. 9.

3. Count Corti, *A History of Smoking* (New York: Harcourt, Brace, 1932), pp. 108–9.

4. B. Mausner and E. Platt, *Smoking: A Behavioral Analysis* (New York: Pergamon Press, 1971), p. 81.

5. John M. Weir, "Male Student Perceptions of Smokers." In *Studies and Issues in Smoking Behavior,* ed. Salvatore V. Zagona (Tucson: University of Arizona Press, 1967), pp. 151–55.

6. Isidor Chein, "Psychological Functions of Drug Use." In *Scientific Basis of Drug Dependence,* ed. Hannah Steinberg (New York: Grune and Stratton, 1969), p. 19.

7. Humphrey Carpenter, *W. H. Auden: A Biography* (London; Boston: George Allen and Unwin, 1981), p. 202.

8. Ibid., p. 43.

9. Sigmund Freud, "Three Essays on Sexuality. Infantile Sexuality." *The Standard Edition of the Complete Psychological Works of Sigmund Freud,* Vol. 7 (London: The Hogarth Press and the Institute of Psycho-Analysis, 1978), p. 182.

10. Desmond Morris, *Intimate Behaviour* (New York: Random House, 1971), p. 195.

11. Charles McArthur et al., "The Psychology of Smoking." *Journal of Abnormal and Social Psychology* 56 (1958), pp. 272–73.

12. Michael Howe and Angela Summerfield, "Orality and Smoking." *British Journal of Medical Psychology* 52 (1979): 85–90.

13. U.S. Patent No. 4,461,309, July 24, 1984. Listed in *Bibliography on Smoking and Health* (U.S. Office on Smoking and Health, 1985), p. 58.

14. B. Heinz, "Cigarette Flavorings: A Key Factor in Brand Distinction." *Tobacco Reporter* 109, no. 10 (October 1982): 52, 56. Listed in *Bibliography on Smoking and Health* (U.S. Office on Smoking and Health, 1983), p. 147.

15. Clark L. Hull, "The Influence of Tobacco Smoking on Mental and Motor Efficiency." *Psychological Monographs* 33, no. 3 (1924): 1–160.

16. Ronald Davis, telephone interview with the author (October 4, 1988).

17. Adam J. Jaffe and Alan G. Glaros, "Taste Dimensions in Cigarette Discrimination: A Multidimensional Scaling Approach." *Addictive Behaviors* 11 (1986): 407–13.

18. Salvatore Zagona and Louis A. Zurcher, Jr., "An Analysis of Some Psychosocial Variables Associated with Smoking Behavior in a College Sample." *Psychological Reports* 17 (1965): 967–78.

19. B. As et al., "Publikums innstilling til roking au filtersigaretter." In *Influencing Smoking Behavior,* ed. J. Wakefield (Geneva: International Union Against Cancer, 1969), p. 16.

20. Jed E. Rose, "The Role of Upper Airway Stimulation in Smoking." In *Nicotine Replacement: A Critical Evaluation,* eds. O. F. Pomerleau and C. S. Pomerleau (New York: Alan R. Liss, 1988), pp. 95–96.

21. K. H. Ginzel, telephone interview with the author (October 17, 1988). See also K. H. Ginzel, "The Lungs as Sites of Origin of Nicotine-induced Skeletomotor Relaxation and Behavioral and Electrocortical Arousal in the Cat." In *Pharmacology of Nicotine,* eds. M. D. Rand and K. Thurau (Oxford; Washington, D.C.: ICSU/IRL Press, 1988), pp. 269–92.

22. Hreday N. Sapru et al., "Stimulation of Pulmonary J Receptors by an Enkephalin-Analog." *Journal of Pharmacology and Experimental Therapeutics* 217, no. 1 (1981): 228–34.

23. Berthold Laufer, *Tobacco and Its Use in Asia,* Leaflet 18 (Chicago: Field Museum of Natural History, 1924), p. 23.

CHAPTER 3

Stimulating People, Putting Elephants to Sleep

1. Fred M. Zackon, *Heroin: The Street Narcotic* (New York: Chelsea House Publications, 1986), p. 24.

2. Joseph Kennedy, *Coca Exotica* (Rutherford; New York: Farleigh Dickinson University Press, Cornwall Books, 1985).

3. Surgeon General's Report, *The Health Consequences of Smoking: Nicotine Addiction* (U.S. Department of Health and Human Services, 1988), pp. 9–10.

4. Zackon, *Heroin: The Street Narcotic,* p. 31.

5. Neal L. Benowitz, "Clinical Pharmacology of Nicotine." *Annual Review of Medicine* 37, (1986), p. 23.

6. Heather Ashton and Rob Stepney, *Smoking: Psychology and Pharmacology* (London; New York: Tavistock Publications, 1983), p. 32.

7. G. L. Mangan and J. F. Golding, *The Psychopharmacology of Smoking* (Cambridge; New York: Cambridge University Press, 1984), p. 103.

8. Surgeon General's Report (1988), p. 595.

9. Murray Jarvik, interview with the author (November 21, 1986).

10. Surgeon General's Report (1988), p. 594.

11. Neal Benowitz, telephone interview with the author (August 11, 1989).

12. Benowitz, "Clinical Pharmacology of Nicotine," p. 24.

13. Jack Henningfield, *Nicotine, An Old-Fashioned Addiction* (New York: Chelsea House Publishers, 1986), p. 76.

14. Surgeon General's Report (1988), p. 10.

15. Jean-Pierre Changeux, *Neuronal Man* (New York: Oxford University Press, 1985), p. 52.

16. Ashton and Stepney, *Smoking: Psychology and Pharmacology,* p. 38.

CHAPTER 4

Staying on an Even Keel

1. T. W. Meade and N. J. Wald, "Cigarette Smoking Patterns During the Working Day." *British Journal of Preventive and Social Medicine* 31 (1977): 25–29.

2. R. Cooperstock and J. Hill, *The Effects of Tranquillization: Benzodiazepine Use in Canada* (Minister of National Health and Welfare, 1982), p. 46.

3. Kenneth Hirsh, "Central Nervous System Pharmacology of the Dietary Methylxanthines." In *The Methylxanthine Beverages and Foods: Chemistry, Consumption and Health Effects,* ed. Gene A. Spiller (New York: Alan R. Liss, 1984), p. 287.

4. N. W. Heimstra, "The Effects of Smoking on Mood Change." In Smoking Behavior: Motives and Incentives, ed. W. L. Dunn (Washington: V. H. Winston and Sons, 1973), pp. 197–207.

5. D. R. Cherek, "Effects of Cigarette Smoking on Human Aggressive Behavior." *Biological Perspectives on Aggression* (1984): 333–44.

6. R. R. Hutchinson and G. S. Emley, "Effects of Nicotine on Avoidance, Conditioned Suppression and Aggression Response Measures in Animals and Man." In Dunn, *Smoking Behavior: Motives and Incentives,* pp. 171–96.

7. Surgeon General's Report (1988), p. 405.

CHAPTER 5

Doing Something With It, Doing Without It

1. Surgeon General's Report (1988), p. 108.

2. Scott E. Lukas, telephone interview with the author (February 9, 1989).

3. Chesire et al., 1973. Cited in Mangan and Golding, *The Psychopharmacology of Smoking,* pp. 125–26.

4. Surgeon General's Report (1988), p. 109.

5. P. M. Cinciripini, "The Effects of Smoking on Electrocortical Arousal in Coronary Prone (Type A) and Non-Coronary Prone (Type B) Subjects." *Psychopharmacology* (Berlin), 90, no. 4 (1986): 522–27.

6. Mangan and Golding, *The Psychopharmacology of Smoking,* p. 127.

7. Lukas, February 9, 1989 interview.

8. Ashton and Stepney, *Smoking: Psychology and Pharmacology,* p. 102.

9. Marianne Frankenhaeuser et al., "Behavioural and Physiological Effects of Cigarette Smoking in a Monotonous Situation." *Psychopharmacologia* 22 (1971): 1–7.

10. D. Gareth Williams, "Effects of Cigarette Smoking on Immediate Memory and Performance in Different Kinds of Smokers." *British Journal of Psychology* 71 (1980): 83–90.

11. Verner J. Knott, "Smoking, EEG and Input Regulation in Smokers and Nonsmokers." In *Smoking Behavior: Physiological and Psychological Influences,* ed. Raymond E. Thornton (Edinburgh; New York: Churchill Livingstone, 1978), p. 116.

12. Verner J. Knott, telephone interview with the author (March 1, 1989). See also Verner J. Knott and Peter H. Venables, "Stimulus Intensity Control and the Cortical Evoked Response in Smokers and Non-Smokers." *Psychophysiology* 15, no. 3 (May 1978), p. 190.

13. Jack Henningfield, principal investigator, "Annual Progress Report: Biology of Dependence and Abuse Potential Assessment Laboratory." In *Annual Report of the Addiction Research Center* (Baltimore: Addiction Research Center, National Institute on Drug Abuse, 1987), and telephone interview with the author (August 3, 1989).

14. Knott, March 1, 1989 interview.

CHAPTER 6
Absolutely

1. K. Wesnes and D. M. Warburton, "Smoking, Nicotine and Human Performance." *Pharmacology and Therapeutics* 21 (1983), pp. 201, 206.

2. Stanley Schachter, "Pharmacological and Psychological Determinants of Smoking." *Annals of Internal Medicine* 88 (1978), p. 106.

3. K. Wesnes and D. M. Warburton, "The Effects of Cigarette Smoking and Nicotine Tablets Upon Human Attention." In Thornton, *Smoking Behavior: Physiological and Psychological Influences,* p. 132.

4. Wesnes and Warburton, "Smoking, Nicotine and Human Performance," p. 204.

5. K. Andersson and G. R. J. Hockey, "Effects of Cigarette Smoking on Incidental Memory." *Psychopharmacologia* 52, no. 3 (1977): 223–26.

6. Verner Knott, "Tobacco Effects on Cortical Evoked Potentials to Distracting Stimuli." *Neuropsychobiology* 13 (1985): 74–80.

7. Verner Knott, "Tobacco Effects on Cortical Evoked Potentials to Task Stimuli." *Addictive Behaviors* 11 (1986): 219–23.

8. Wesnes and Warburton, "Smoking, Nicotine and Human Performance," p. 197.

9. Ibid. See also K. Wesnes and D. M. Warburton, "Effects of Scopolamine and Nicotine on Human Rapid Information Processing Performance." *Psychopharmacology* 82 (1984): 147–50.

10. Dick Waller and Sten Levander, "Smoking and Vigilance." *Psychopharmacology* 70 (1980), p. 131.

11. K. M. Warwick and H. J. Eysenck, "Experimental Studies of the Behavioural Effects of Nicotine." *Pharmakopsychiatrie Neuro-Psychopharmakologie* 1 (1968): 145–69.

12. R. J. West and M. J. Jarvis, "Effects of Nicotine on Finger-Tapping Rate in Non-smokers." *Pharmacology, Biochemistry and Behavior* 25 (1986): 727–31.

13. G. N. Connolly et al., "Use of Smokeless Tobacco in Major-League Baseball." *New England Journal of Medicine* 318, no. 19 (1988): 1281–85.

14. Steven W. Edwards et al., "The Effects of Smokeless Tobacco on Heart Rate and Neuromuscular Reactivity in Athletes and Nonathletes." *The Physician and Sportsmedicine* 15, no. 7 (July 1987): 141–47.

15. Jeannette Friedman and Russell Meares, "Tobacco Smoking and Cortical Evoked Potentials: An Opposite Effect on Auditory and Visual Systems." *Clinical and Experimental Pharmacology and Physiology* 7 (1980), p. 613.

16. Phillip Woodson, telephone interview with the author (August 15, 1989), and Phillip P. Woodson et al., "Effects of Nicotine on the Visual Evoked Response." *Pharmacology, Biochemistry and Behavior* 17 (1982): 915–20.

17. Surgeon General's Report (1988), p. 429. The report contains an excellent review of this topic through 1987, from which much of my account is taken.

18. Ibid., p. 432.

19. Kenneth A. Perkins et al., "The Effect of Nicotine on Energy Expenditure During Light Physical Activity." *New England Journal of Medicine* 320, no. 14 (April 6, 1989): 898–903.

20. Larry A. Tucker, "Cigarette Smoking Intentions and Obesity among High School Males." *Psychological Reports* 52 (April 1983): 530.

21. Anne Charlton, "Smoking and Weight control in Teenagers." *Public Health* (London), 98 (1984): 277–81. Cited in the Surgeon General's Report (1988), p. 436.

22. R. C. Klesges et al., "An Evaluation of Demographic, Attitudinal, and Health Knowledge Variables on Smoking Status." Cited in the Surgeon General's Report (1988), p. 437.

23. Robert Klesges, "An Analysis of Body Image Distortions in a Nonpatient Population." *International Journal of Eating Disorders* 2, no. 2 (Winter 1983): 35–41.

24. Phil Gunby, "Seeking to End Smoking's Appeal to Women, Youth." *Journal of the American Medical Association* 253, no. 20 (May 24–31, 1985), p. 2943.

CHAPTER 7
Controlling the Ship's Captain

1. Interview by the author with Josselyn, middle-aged woman, Berkeley, California (November 1988).

2. Jerome Jaffe, in *The Pharmacological Basis of Therapeutics*, eds. Alfred Goodman Gilman and Louis S. Goodman (New York: Macmillan, 1980), pp. 547–48.

3. See especially the Surgeon General's Report (1988), Chapter 4.

4. L. Kozlowski et al., "Nicotine Yields of Cigarettes, Plasma Nicotine in Smokers, and Public Health." *Preventive Medicine* 11 (1982), p. 242.

5. Neal L. Benowitz, "Health and Public Policy Implications of the 'Low Yield' Cigarette." (Editorial) *New England Journal of Medicine* 320, no. 24 (June 15, 1989): 1619–21.

6. S. R. Goldberg et al., "Persistent Behavior at High Rates Maintained by Intravenous Self-administration of Nicotine." *Science* 214, no. 4520 (October 30, 1981): 573–75.

7. Jack E. Henningfield et al., "Cigarette Smokers Self-administer Intravenous Nicotine." *Pharmacology, Biochemistry and Behavior* 19 (November 1983): 887–90.

8. D. R. Jasinski et al., "Abuse Liability Assessment in Human Subjects." *Trends in Pharmacological Science* 5 (May 1984): 196–200. J. E. Henningfield et al., "Abuse Liability and Pharmacodynamic Characteristics of Intravenous and Inhaled Nicotine." *Journal of Pharmacology and Experimental Therapeutics* 234, no. 1 (1985): 1–12.

9. D. K. Hatsukami et al., "Tobacco Withdrawal Symptoms: An Experimental Analysis." *Psychopharmacology* 84 (1984): 231–36.

10. J. R. Hughes and D. K. Hatsukami, "Signs and Symptoms of Tobacco Withdrawal." *Archives of General Psychiatry* 43 (March 1986): 289–94.

11. D. Hatsukami, J. R. Hughes, and R. Pickens, "Characterization of Tobacco Withdrawal: Physiological and Subjective Effects." *Pharmacological Adjuncts in Smoking Cessation*, NIDA Research Monograph 53, eds. John Grabowski and Sharon M. Hall (U.S. Department of Health and Human Services, 1985), pp. 56–67.

12. Hughes and Hatsukami, "Signs and Symptoms of Tobacco Withdrawal," p. 292.

13. Surgeon General's Report (1988), p. 200.

14. M. A. H. Russell, "Smoking Problems: An Overview." In *Research on Smoking Behavior,* NIDA Research Monograph 17, eds. Murray Jarvik et al. (U.S. Department of Health and Human Services, 1977), pp. 18–19.

15. W. A. Hunt et al., "Relapse Rates in Addiction Programs." *Journal of Clinical Psychology* 27, no. 4 (October 1971), p. 456.

16. Stanley Schachter, "Recidivism and Self-Cure of Smoking and Obesity." *American Psychologist* 37, no. 4 (April 1982): 436–44. M. A. Russell, "The Nicotine Addiction Trap: A 40-year Sentence for Four Cigarettes." *British Journal of Addiction* 85, no. 2 (February 1990): 293–300.

CHAPTER 8
Inside the Black Box

1. D. J. Greenblatt and R. I. Shader, "Effects of Age and Other Drugs on Benzodiazepine Kinetics." Cited in Cooperstock and Hill, *The Effects of Tranquillization: Benzodiazepine Use in Canada,* p. 21.

2. Solomon Snyder, *Drugs and the Brain* (New York: Scientific American Books, 1986), pp. 84–86.

3. Roy A. Wise, "The Neurobiology of Craving: Implications for the Understanding and Treatment of Addiction." *Journal of Abnormal Psychology* 97, no. 2 (1988): 118–32.

4. Agu Pert and Paul B. S. Clark, "Nicotinic Modulation of Dopaminergic Neurotransmission: Functional Implications." In *Tobacco Smoking and Nicotine: A Neurobiological Approach,* eds. William R. Martin et al. (New York: Plenum Press, 1987), pp. 169–189. G. DiChara and A. Imperato, "Drugs Abused by Humans Preferentially Increase Synaptic Dopamine Concentrations in the Mesolimbic System of Freely Moving Rats." *Proceedings of the National Academy of Sciences* 85, no. 14 (July 1988): 5274–78.

5. Wise, "The Neurobiology of Craving," p. 127.

6. Roy A. Wise, "The Role of Reward Pathways in the Development of Drug Dependence." *Pharmacology and Therapeutics* 35 (1987), p. 250.

CHAPTER 9
Gimme That Stuff

1. Robert Hughes, *The Fatal Shore* (New York: Vintage Books, 1988), p. 380.

2. N. A. Photiades, letter, *Times* of London (July 5, 1957), p. 11.

3. F. I. Arntzen, "Some Psychological Aspects of Nicotinism." *The American Journal of Psychology* 61, no. 3 (July 1948): 424–25.

CHAPTER 10

The Threads of Addiction

1. H. H. Blumberg et al., 1974. Cited in Russell, "The Smoking Habit," p. 791.

2. Lynn Kozlowski, telephone interview with the author (October 28, 1987).

3. Harbans Lal et al., "Alleviation of Narcotic Withdrawal Syndrome by Conditional Stimulus." *Pavlovian Journal of Biological Science* 11, no. 4 (October-December 1976): 251–62.

4. G. L. Mangan and J. Golding, "An 'Enhancement' Model of Smoking Maintenance?" Cited in Ashton and Stepney, *Smoking: Psychology and Pharmacology*, p. 159.

5. Raymond S. Niaura et al., "Relevance of Cue Reactivity to Understanding Alcohol and Smoking Relapse." *Journal of Abnormal Psychology* 97, no. 2 (1988): 133–52.

CHAPTER 11

The Personality of Smoking

1. On seat belt wearing and binge drinking: Patrick Remington et al., "Current Smoking Trends in the United States: The 1981–1983 Behavioral Risk Factor Surveys." *Journal of the American Medical Association* 253, no. 20 (May 24–31, 1985): 2975–2978. On downward mobility: Leo G. Reeder, "Sociocultural Factors in the Etiology of Smoking Behavior: An Assessment." In Jarvik et al., *Research on Smoking Behavior*, p. 194.

2. Dorothy E. Green, "Patterns of Tobacco Use in the United States." In *Cigarette Smoking as a Dependence Process*, NIDA Research Monograph 23, ed. Norman Krasnegor (U.S. Department of Health, Education and Welfare, 1979), p. 48.

3. G. M. Smith, "Personality and Smoking: A Review of the Empirical Literature." In Hunt, *Learning Mechanisms in Smoking*, p. 47.

4. See L. T. Kozlowski, "Psychological Influences on Cigarette Smoking." In *The Behavioral Aspects of Smoking*, NIDA Research Monograph 26, ed. Norman A. Krasnegor (U.S. Department of Health, Education and Welfare, 1979), pp. 101–103.

5. John R. Hughes et al., "Prevalence of Smoking Among Psychiatric Outpatients." *American Journal of Psychiatry* 143, no. 8 (August 1986): 993–97.

6. Alexander H. Glassman et al., "Heavy Smokers, Smoking Cessation, and Clonidine." *Journal of the American Medical Association* 259, no. 19 (May 20, 1988): 2863–66.

7. Alexander H. Glassman et al., "Smoking, Smoking Cessation, and Major Depression." *Journal of the American Medical Association* 264, no. 12 (September 26, 1990: 1546–49.

8. Robert F. Anda et al., "Depression and the Dynamics of Smoking." *Journal of the American Medical Association* 264, no. 12 (September 26, 1990): 1541–45.

9. Leo Tolstoy, *Why Do Men Stupefy Themselves? and Other Writings,* trans. Aylmer Maude, eds. Meredith Murray and the Editors of 24 Magazine (Hankins, N.Y.: Strength Books, 1975) pp. 55–56.

10. H. J. Eysenck, *Smoking, Health and Personality* (New York: Basic Books, 1965), p. 80.

11. Ibid.

12. H. J. Eysenck, "Personality and the Maintenance of the Smoking Habit." In Dunn, *Smoking Behavior: Motives and Incentives,* p. 122. Eysenck, *Smoking, Health and Personality,* p. 84.

13. Robert M. Stelmack, "Biological Bases of Extraversion: Psychophysiological Evidence." *Journal of Personality* 58, no. 1 (March 1990): 293–311.

14. Barry D. Smith, "Extraversion and Electrodermal Activity: Arousability and the Inverted-U." *Personality and Individual Differences* 4, no. 4 (1983), p. 411.

15. H. J. Eysenck et al., "Sport and Personality." *Advances in Behavior Research and Therapy* 4 (1982): 1–56.

16. Smith, "Extraversion and Electrodermal Activity."

17. Stelmack, "Biological Bases of Extraversion," p. 302.

18. Associated Press Story in the San Francisco *Chronicle* (March 11, 1987), p. 1.

19. H. J. Eysenck, "A Note on 'Smoking Personality and Reasons for Smoking.'" *Psychological Medicine* 13 (1983): 447–448.

CHAPTER 12
The Motivation That Precedes Us

1. Surgeon General's Report (1988), p. 566.

2. J. Shields. Cited in S. S. Kety, "The Motivational Factors in Cigarette Smoking: A Summary." In Dunn, *Smoking Behavior: Motives and Incentives,* pp. 293–94.

3. J. R. Hughes, "Genetics of Smoking: A Brief Review." *Behavior Therapy* 17 (1986): 335–45.

4. H. J. Eysenck and L. J. Eaves. Cited in Hughes, "Genetics of Smoking," p. 336.

5. Surgeon General's Report (1988), p. 506.

6. Murray C. Hannah et al., "Twin Concordance for a Binary Trait. II. Nested Analysis of Ever-Smoking and Ex-Smoking Traits and Unnested Analysis of a 'Committed-Smoking' Trait." *American Journal of Human Genetics* 37 (1985): 153–65.

7. H. J. Eysenck, "Genetic and Environmental Contributions to Individual Differences: The Three Major Dimensions of Personality." *Journal of Personality* 58, no. 1 (March 1990): 245–61. Thomas J. Bouchard, Jr., et al., "Sources of Human Psychological Differences: The Minnesota Study of Twins Reared Apart." *Science* 250 (October 12, 1990): 223–28.

8. Bouchard, et al., "Sources of Human Psychological Differences," p. 227.

CHAPTER 13

In and Out of Dracula's Lair

1. Stanton Peele, *The Meaning of Addiction: Compulsive Experience and Its Interpretation* (Lexington, Mass.: Lexington Books, D. C. Heath and Company, 1985), p. 28.

2. Marty Mann, *Primer on Alcoholism* (New York: Rinehart, 1950). Cited in Herbert Fingarette, *Heavy Drinking: The Myth of Alcoholism as a Disease* (Berkeley: University of California Press, 1988), p. 31.

3. Mark Keller, "On the Loss-of-Control Phenomenon in Alcoholism." *British Journal of Addiction* 67 (1972): 153–66. Cited in Fingarette, *Heavy Drinking*, p. 33.

4. Fingarette, *Heavy Drinking*, p. 42.

5. Ronald Melzack, "The Tragedy of Needless Pain." *Scientific American* 262, no. 2 (February 1990): 27–33.

6. Lee N. Robins et al., "Narcotic Use in Southeast Asia and Afterward." *Archives of General Psychiatry* 32 (1975): 955–61.

7. Norman Zinberg and Richard Jacobson, "The Natural History of 'Chipping.'" *American Journal of Psychiatry* 133, no. 1 (January 1976), p. 40.

8. Fingarette, *Heavy Drinking*, p. 100.

9. Peele, *The Meaning of Addiction,* p. 103.

10. Marc A. Schuckit, *Drug and Alcohol Abuse,* 3d ed. (New York: Plenum Medical Book Company, 1989), p. 65.

11. C. C. Allcock, "Pathological Gambling." *Australian and New Zealand Journal of Psychiatry* 20 (1986): 259–65.

12. Agnes Whitaker et al., "Uncommon Troubles in Young People: Prevalence Estimates of Selected Psychiatric Disorders in a Nonreferred Adolescent Population." *Archives of General Psychiatry* 47, no. 5 (1990): 487–96.

13. Richard Benyo, "The Perils of Exercise Addiction," San Francisco *Chronicle,* January 21, 1991, p. E-1, and telephone interview with the author (February 12, 1991).

14. Chein, "Psychological Functions of Drug Use." In Steinberg, *Scientific Basis of Drug Dependence.* Cited in Peele, *The Meaning of Addiction,* pp. 112–113.

15. S. Peele with A. Brodsky, *Love and Addiction* (New York: Taplinger, 1975). Cited in Peele, *The Meaning of Addiction,* p. 157.

16. Stanton Peele, *Diseasing of America: Addiction Treatment Out of Control* (Lexington, Mass.: Lexington Books, D. C. Heath and Company, 1989), p. 273.

17. Surgeon General's Report (1988), p. 572.

18. Murray E. Jarvik, "The Drug Dilemma: Manipulating the Demand." *Science* 250 (October 19, 1990), p. 387.

APPENDIX

Advice on Quitting

Since this is a practical appendix, I wanted to do away with the clutter of citation references. I would, however, like to note some authors whose research data and analysis were particularly helpful to me. They are:

1. Timothy P. Carmody, "Preventing Relapse in the Treatment of Nicotine Addiction: Current Issues and Future Directions." *Journal of Psychoactive Drugs* 22, no. 2 (April–June 1990): 211–38.

2. Sheldon Cohen et al., "Debunking Myths About Self-Quitting." *American Psychologist* 44, no. 11 (November 1989): 1355–65.

3. H. Catherina Coppotelli and C. Tracy Orleans, "Partner Support and Other Determinants of Smoking Cessation Maintenance Among Women." *Journal of Consulting and Clinical Psychology* 53, no. 4 (1985): 455–60.

4. Carlyle H. Folkins and Wesley E. Sime, "Physical Fitness Training and Mental Health." *American Psychologist* 36, no. 4 (April 1981): 373–89.

5. R. M. Foxx and Richard A. Brown, "Nicotine Fading and Self-Monitoring for Cigarette Abstinence or Controlled Smoking." *Journal of Applied Behavior Analysis* 12 (Spring 1979): 111–25.

6. Jack E. Henningfield et al., "Drinking Coffee and Carbonated Beverages Blocks Absorption of Nicotine from Nicotine Polacrilex Gum." *Journal of the American Medical Association* 264, no. 12 (September 26, 1990): 1560–64.

7. G. Alan Marlatt and Judith R. Gordon, eds., *Relapse Prevention: Maintenance Strategies in the Treatment of Addictive Behaviors* (New York: Guilford Press, 1985). I recommend this book both for its general treatment of the subject of addictive relapse and for Saul Shiffman and colleague's chapter on preventing relapse in ex-smokers.

8. R. M. Nicki et al., "Self-Efficacy, Nicotine-Fading/Self-Monitoring and Cigarette-Smoking Behaviour." *Behavioral Research Therapy* 22, no. 5 (1984): 477–85.

9. Saul Shiffman: Many publications, but a good summary of his work with the Stay-Quit Line project is contained in T. Loberg et al., eds., *Addictive Behaviors: Prevention and Early Intervention* (Amsterdam: Swets and Zeitlinger, 1989).

10. Clearing the Air, NIH Publication 89-1647 (U.S. Department of Health and Human Services, 1989).

11. Surgeon General's Report, *The Health Consequences of Smoking: Nicotine Addiction* (U.S. Department of Health and Human Services, 1988). See particularly Chapter 7, "Treatment of Tobacco Dependence."

Index

acetylcholine (ACH), 32–34, 49, 84
addiction, as concept, 140
    theories of, 124–125
additives, cigarette, 18–19n
adolescent smoking rates, girls/boys, 69, 101
adrenaline (epinephrine), 32
advertising, cigarette, 14–15, 17–18, 37, 69, 114
airway stimulation, tobacco, 21–26
alcoholism, 3, 78, 80, 87
    central activity model of, 129–130
    through history, 27, 131
    disease model of, 124–127
    prevalence estimate of, 132

    relapse to, 80
Alcoholics Anonymous, 126
Alzheimer's disease, 140
American Cancer Society, 146
American Lung Association, 146
amphetamines, 33, 43, 49, 53, 85
Anda, Robert, 105
Andersson, Karin, 59
anorexia nervosa, prevalence, 132
Arntzen, F. I., 91
arousal, 48–51, 62, 120
    relation to personality, 108–111
Ashton, Heather, 52
Auden, W. H., 15–16, 96
axon, definition, 31